HOUGHTON MIFFLIN
ENGLISH

Shirley Haley-James   John Warren Stewig

Kenneth William Bierly
Jacqueline L. Chaparro
Helen Felsenthal
Norman A. Felsenthal
Michael C. Flanigan

Mary Mercer Krogness
Harry D. Laub
Nancy C. Millett
Paula J. Parris
Judy Griswold Parsons

Joy Harris Schlagal
Robert C. Schlagal
June Grant Shane
Helen J. Throckmorton

HOUGHTON MIFFLIN COMPANY · BOSTON
Atlanta · Dallas · Geneva, Illinois · Hopewell, New Jersey · Palo Alto · Toronto

Acknowledgments

Dictionary entries, reprinted from *My First Dictionary* by permission of Houghton Mifflin Company. © 1980 Houghton Mifflin Company.

"Dos y Dos Son Cuatro," from *Play It In Spanish: Spanish Games and Folk Songs for Children,* collected and translated by Mariana Prieto. Musical arrangement by Elizabeth Colwell Nielsen. A John Day Book. Copyright © 1973 by Harper & Row, Publishers, Inc. Reprinted by permission of Thomas Y. Crowell, Publishers.

"Jet" and "Flower" word collages, and "Ride, ride, ride your bike," from *Growing from Word Play into Poetry,* by Buff Bradley. Copyright © 1976. Reprinted by permission of Pitman Learning, Inc., Belmont, California.

"My House," by Jane W. Krows. Extensive research failed to locate the copyright holder of this selection.

"Oh, Who Will Wash the Tiger's Ears?" by Shel Silverstein, from *The Book of Giggles,* collected by William Cole. World Publishing Company. Copyright © 1967 by Shel Silverstein. Reprinted by permission of William Cole for Shel Silverstein.

"Quoits," by Mary Effie Lee Newsome, from *Golden Slippers,* edited by Arna Bontemps. Copyright 1941 by Harper & Row, Publishers, Inc. Reprinted by permission of the publisher.

Two riddles ("bird" and "elephant") from *It Does Not Say Meow and Other Animal Riddle Rhymes,* by Beatrice Schenk de Regniers. Copyright © 1972 by Beatrice Schenk de Regniers. Reprinted by permission of Clarion Books, Ticknor & Fields: A Houghton Mifflin Company, New York.

Credits

Cover and Title Page Photography by Olmsted Studio

Illustration

Lorinda Bryan Cauley: pp. 135, 136, 137, 138, 139, 140, 141, 142 (bottom right), 144, 148, 149, 150, 151, 152 (left), 153, 155.

Linda Chen: pp. 19, 39, 40, 67, 93, 120.

Lynne Cherry: pp. 10, 11, 12, 13, 14, 16, 17, 18, 21, 22, 23, 24, 25, 26, 27, 28, 29, 30, 31, 32, 33, 34, 35, 36, 37, 38, 53, 54, 55, 56, 57, 60, 61, 62, 63, 64, 65, 66, 80, 81, 82, 83 (top), 84, 85, 86, 87, 88, 89, 90, 91, 92, 94, 107, 108, 109, 110, 112, 113, 115, 116, 117, 118, 119.

Eileen Christelow: pp. 97, 98, 99, 100, 101, 102, 103, 104, 124, 125, 126, 127, 128, 129, 130, 131, 132, 133.

Jane Dyer: pp. 43, 44, 45, 46, 47, 48, 49, 50, 51.

David Kelley: pp. 105, 142, 143, 147, 150 (middle), 152 (right), 154.

Diana Magnuson: pp. 69, 70, 71, 72, 73, 74, 75, 76, 77.

George M. Ulrich: pp. 111, 114.

Handwriting by Mark Mulhall.

Photography

Elliott Erwitt/Magnum: p. 8 (top); Arnold Zann/Black Star: p. 8 (bottom left); Gabor Demjen/Stock, Boston: p. 8 (bottom right); John Lewis Stage/Image Bank: p. 20; Elizabeth Crews/Stock, Boston: p. 42; John Lewis Stage/Image Bank: p. 52; Bill Binzen: p. 68; Clyde Smith/Peter Arnold: p. 78; David K. Smith: p. 79; David K. Smith: p. 83; Peter F. Runyon/Image Bank: p. 96; Gregg Mancuso/After Image: p. 106; Elizabeth Crews: p. 122; Harold Krieger/Image Bank: p. 134; John Launois/Black Star: p. 146.

Contents

Unit 1 | Sentences   **Page 8**

1	Talk and Listen	9
2	The Sentence	10
3	Word Order in Sentences	12
4	Telling Sentences and Questions	14
5	Sentence Parts	16
6	Sign Talk	18
	REVIEW	19

Unit 2 | Naming Words   **Page 20**

1	Talking About Yourself	21
2	Naming Words	22
3	One and More than One	24
4	Using is and are	26
5	Special Names	28
6	Titles for People	30
7	Days and Months	31
8	Writing Months a Short Way	33
9	Dates	35
10	Holidays	37
11	Compound Words	38
	REVIEW	39

Unit 3 | Writing a Class Story

Page 42

1 Getting Started   43
2 Choose an Idea   44
3 Write the Class Story   45
4 Revise the Class Story   46
5 Make a Final Copy   48
6 Proofread the Class Story   50

Unit 4 | Action Words

Page 52

1 Calling for Help   53
2 Action Words   54
3 Adding -ed to Verbs   56
4 Using did, done, gave, given   58
5 Using saw, seen, went, gone   60
6 Using ran, run, came, come   62
7 don't, doesn't, isn't, can't   64
8 Words That Name Noises   66
  REVIEW   67

Unit 5 | Writing About Yourself

Page 68

1 Getting Started   69
2 Choose a Story   70
3 Write Your Story   71
4 Revise Your Story   73
5 Proofread Your Story   75
6 Make a Final Copy   77

Unit 6 | Describing Things **Page 78**

1	Talking About Things	79
2	Words That Describe	80
3	Words That Compare	83
4	Correct Order	85
5	Directions	86
6	Maps	89
7	Opposites	92
	REVIEW	93

Unit 7 | Writing a Description **Page 96**

1	Getting Started	97
2	Choose an Idea	99
3	Write Your Description	100
4	Revise Your Description	101
5	Proofread Your Description	103
6	Make a Final Copy	105

Unit 8 | Working with Words **Page 106**

1	ABC Order	107
2	The Dictionary	110
3	Finding Word Meanings	113
4	Getting the Meaning	116
5	More than One Meaning	118
	REVIEW	120

Unit 9 | Writing a Letter — Page 122

1	Parts of a Letter	123
2	Getting Started	125
3	Choose an Idea	126
4	Write Your Letter	127
5	Revise Your Letter	128
6	Proofread Your Letter	130
7	Make a Final Copy	
	Address an Envelope	132

Unit 10 | Literature — Page 134

1	Rhyme	135
2	Rhythm	138
3	Music	140
4	Special Poems	142
5	Riddles	144

Unit 11 | Sharing Books — Page 146

1	Making a Picture Report	147
2	Making a Picture Postcard	150
3	Making a Book Jacket	152
4	Making Riddles	154
Words for Writing		156
Index		159

UNIT 1 Sentences

1 | Talk and Listen

Look at the children on page 8. What are they doing? What do you think they can see and hear?

Pretend you are visiting one place you see on page 8. What is happening around you? What can you see and hear? What are you doing? Is anyone with you? Make up a story about your visit.

Try It Out

Tell your story to the class. Tell these things.

Tell which place you visited.
Tell who was there.
Tell what you saw and heard.
Tell what was happening.
Tell what you did.

Wait your turn to tell your story. Talk clearly so that everyone will understand you. When others tell their stories, listen carefully to what they say.

Take turns telling things.
Listen when others talk.
Talk clearly so that everyone will understand you.

2 | The Sentence

Look at the groups of words below. The groups of words are <u>sentences</u>.

The frog leaped into the air.
It jumped over a big log.

The words in a sentence must make sense. A sentence begins with a capital letter.

Try It Out

Read these groups of words aloud.

in books.
The frog splashed in the water.

Tell which group of words is a sentence. The group of words must make sense and begin with a capital letter.

> ▸ A **sentence** is a group of words that makes sense.
> Begin a sentence with a capital letter.

Practice

Find the sentences. Write them.

1. The rockets are yellow.
2. very tall.
3. Rockets can fly very fast.
4. flying to a big star.
5. They will not land on the moon.
6. The rockets will go today.
7. hot sun.
8. People will watch them.

- **Write a Sentence** Write a sentence about something you see in this picture.

Read your sentence carefully. Does it make sense?
Does it begin with a capital letter?

3 | Word Order in Sentences

Look at the two groups of words below. The words are the same, but they are not in the same order.

The small look stars.
The stars look small.

The words in a sentence must be in an order that makes sense. Which group of words above is a sentence?

Try It Out

A. Read these groups of words aloud. Tell which groups are sentences. Are the words in an order that makes sense?

1. We are in a spaceship.
2. Flying to we are the moon.
3. Fast flying the is spaceship.
4. We will land on the moon.

B. Put these groups of words in an order that makes sense. Tell what they say.

1. Sky dark the is.
2. See moon we the can.
3. Looks the moon yellow.
4. Above trees the moon the is.
5. Round the moon is.

> The words in a sentence must be in an order that makes sense.

Practice

A. Look at these groups of words. Find the sentences. Write them.

1. Hungry the was brown mouse little.
2. The mouse nibbled some seeds.
3. It took a drink of cold water.
4. Saw mouse a cat big the.
5. The mouse dashed into a hole.

B. Use the words below to make a sentence. Put them in an order that makes sense. Write the sentence.

the rolled mud in the pig

Now read your sentence carefully. Are the words in an order that makes sense? Does the sentence begin with a capital letter?

- **Write a Sentence** Use the words in the box to make a sentence. Write your sentence.

> red on
> the a
> jumps
> bug
> flower

4 | Telling Sentences and Questions

The sentences below tell something. They are **telling sentences**. A telling sentence ends with a period.

Mr. Worm climbed into his boat.
He was going fishing.

The sentences below ask something. They are called **questions**. A question ends with a question mark.

Will the boat go?
What will Mr. Worm catch?

Try It Out

A. These children are talking about the picture. Read aloud what they are saying. Which sentence is a question? Which sentence tells?

Who is in the balloon?

The bears are in the balloon.

B. Look again at the picture of the bears riding in the balloon.

    1. Say a telling sentence about the picture.
    2. Ask a question about the picture.

> ▶ **Sentences** tell something or ask a question.
> End telling sentences with a period.
> End questions with a question mark.

Practice

Write these sentences. Put a period at the end of sentences that tell. Put a question mark at the end of questions.

    1. Mrs. Giraffe is a pilot ____
    2. She loves to fly ____
    3. Will Mrs. Hippo fly with her ____
    4. Where will she go ____

• **Write Sentences** Write one telling sentence and one question about this picture. Begin each sentence with a capital letter. Put a period or a question mark at the end of each sentence.

5 | Sentence Parts

Look at these sentences.

> A small door flew open.
> A red fox walked out the door.

The part that is underlined is the beginning of the sentence. **Sentence beginnings** tell who or what is being talked about.

Look at these sentences.

> Mr. Fox entered the star ship.
> The star ship lifted off the ground.

The part that is underlined is the sentence ending. **Sentence endings** tell what is happening or is being done.

Try It Out

A. End these sentences. Tell what happens or is done.

1. Captain Carrot _____.
2. Twelve tall tigers _____.

B. Begin these sentences. Tell who or what is being talked about.

1. _____ wiggled its nose.
2. _____ buzzed in my ear.

A sentence has two parts. It has a beginning and an ending.

Practice

A. Read these sentence endings. Think of a beginning for each one. Tell who or what is being talked about. Write your sentences.

1. _____ peeked over the wall.
2. _____ crawled into the bag.

B. Read these sentence beginnings. Think of an ending for each one. Tell what happens or what is done. Write your sentences.

1. The magic frog _____.
2. The secret hiding hole _____.

- **Write a Sentence** Choose a sentence beginning and a sentence ending from the box. Make a sentence. Write it.

did three flips	grew under a tree
the wiggly pig	one brown mushroom

Read your sentence carefully. Does it begin with a capital letter? Are the words in an order that makes sense? Does it end with a period?

6 | Sign Talk

Signs are everywhere. You use them all the time. Signs tell you things. They can help you.

There are many different kinds of signs. Some signs say things with words. Other signs say things with just pictures. Some signs say things with pictures and words.

People can make signs, too. They can make signs with their hands and with their faces.

Try It Out

Look at these signs. What are they telling you?

 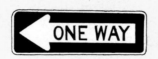

Look at these hand signs. What are they telling you?

Practice

- **Write a Sentence**   Write a sentence that tells what this sign means to you.

A. Read these groups of words. Write the sentences.

   1. Our spaceship is ready.   **3.** When are we going?
   2. is on the   **4.** We fast going are.

B. Look at the words in the box. Use the words to make a telling sentence. Write your sentence.

tiger	sleeping	the	is

C. Look at the words in the box. Use the words to make a question. Write your question.

kitten	the	is	where

D. Write these sentences. Put the correct mark at the end of each sentence.

   1. It is raining ____   **3.** Is the dog muddy ____
   2. The streets are wet ____   **4.** Did you get wet ____

E. Think of a beginning or an ending for these sentences. Write the sentences you make.

   1. The man on the bus ____.
   2. ____ will go in the morning.

Naming Words

1 | Talking About Yourself

When you talk about someone else and yourself, say the name of the other person first. Whose name comes first in these sentences?

Jimmy and I rode our new bikes.
Then Robin and I flew kites.

When you talk about another person and yourself, name the other person first.

Try It Out

A. Look at these sentences. Which sentence names another person first? Read that sentence aloud.

1. I and Andy love to play marbles.
2. Andy and I will play after lunch.

B. Answer these questions. Talk about you and your best friend. Say your friend's name. Say your name last.

1. What do the two of you do after school?
2. What do the two of you do on Saturday?
3. What is your favorite thing to do together?

2 | Naming Words

A word that names something is a **naming word**. A naming word names a person, place, or thing. Naming words are called **nouns**.

Read these sentences. The underlined words are nouns.

Come to the <u>game</u>.
My <u>friend</u> is coming.
The <u>boys</u> are not going.
We will meet by the <u>swings</u>.

Try It Out

A. Read each sentence aloud. Find the naming word and tell it. The naming word is a noun.

1. A horn blew.
2. The game began.
3. The players ran.
4. People cheered.
5. The band played.
6. Our team won.

B. Finish each sentence. Use a noun. Tell your sentence aloud.

1. Let's go to the _____.
2. I want to play on the _____.
3. We can take our _____.
4. The _____ can come with us.
5. Everyone can climb on the _____.

> ▶ A **naming word** names a person, a place, or a thing.
> ▶ A naming word is called a **noun**.

Practice

A. Write each sentence. Use a noun in the blank. Remember that a noun is a naming word.

1. The _____ started on time.
2. Players tossed the _____ into the air.
3. The teams played in the _____.
4. Our team wore red _____.

B. Read this sign. Write the nouns. Nouns are naming words.

> **The Game**
> Come see the teachers play.
> Get your tickets at the door.
> Bring your family and friends.

• **Write a Sentence** Write a sentence about this picture. Use nouns in your sentence. Circle the nouns.

3 | One and More than One

Nouns can name <u>one</u> person, place, or thing. Nouns can also name <u>more than one</u> person, place, or thing.

Look at the underlined nouns in these sentences. Each underlined noun in the first sentence names one thing. The underlined nouns in the second sentence name more than one thing.

> The <u>horse</u> ate the <u>carrot</u>.
> <u>Horses</u> love to eat <u>carrots</u>.

What letter was added to <u>horse</u> to make <u>horses</u>? What letter was added to <u>carrot</u> to make <u>carrots</u>? Most nouns add <u>-s</u> to show more than one.

Try It Out

A. Look at each underlined noun. Tell if it means one or more than one.

1. The <u>swimmers</u> are ready for the <u>race</u>.
2. They will jump in the <u>pool</u> when the <u>bell</u> rings.
3. <u>Ribbons</u> will go to the <u>winners</u>.

hammer
seeds
hose
ladder
rake
pail
gloves
flowers

B. Mary's dad made a list of things he needs to buy. Look at his list. Say each word that means one. Then tell what letter to add to it to make it mean more than one.

> Add -s to most nouns to show more than one.

Practice

A. Read this story. Write all the nouns that mean more than one.

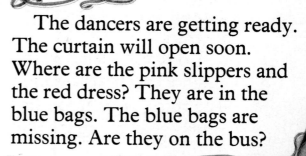

The dancers are getting ready. The curtain will open soon. Where are the pink slippers and the red dress? They are in the blue bags. The blue bags are missing. Are they on the bus?

B. Read these sentences. Find the noun or nouns in each sentence. Think how to change them to mean more than one. Write the new words.

1. The girl picked up the ball.
2. She grabbed the bat and mitt.
3. She put on her hat.
4. She dashed to the park.
5. The game had just started.

- **Write a Sentence** Choose one noun you wrote above. Write a sentence using that noun.

4 | Using is and are

Read these sentences. Look at the underlined words.

One pot is blue.
A cup is cracked.

One pot is blue and one cup is cracked. When you talk about one person, place, or thing, use the word is.

Read these sentences. Look at the underlined words.

Three pots are purple.
All the cups are orange.

More than one pot is purple. More than one cup is orange. When you talk about more than one person, place, or thing, use the word are.

Try It Out

Complete each sentence. Say is or are.

1. All the pots _____ finished.
2. One pot _____ on the table.
3. Some pots _____ near the clay.
4. A cracked cup _____ on the shelf.

> Use is when talking about <u>one</u> person, place, or thing.
> Use <u>are</u> when talking about <u>more than one</u> person, place, or thing.

Practice

A. Write these sentences. Use <u>is</u> or <u>are</u> correctly.

1. The cans (is, are) filled with water.
2. The paintbrushes (is, are) on the table.
3. The teacher (is, are) looking for the paint.
4. Do you know where the jar (is, are)?

B. Write each sentence. Use <u>is</u> or <u>are</u> correctly.

1. The puppet show ____ this afternoon.
2. Our friends ____ coming.
3. All the puppets ____ made.
4. The big, spotted dragon ____ my favorite.

• **Write Sentences**   Write a sentence for each picture. Use <u>is</u> or <u>are</u> in each sentence.

Ben ____

The girls ____

5 | Special Names

Read this story. Look at the underlined nouns. These nouns name a special person, place, and pet. The names of special people, places, and pets begin with capital letters.

There was a man named <u>Dean</u>.
He lived in <u>Lakewood</u>.
He had a pet dog named <u>Wags</u>.

Try It Out

A. Read these sentences aloud. Find the nouns in each sentence. Remember that a noun is a naming word. Tell which noun in each sentence names a special person, place, or pet. What kind of letter begins a special name?

1. Honeytown had a big parade.
2. Wendy played the drums in the band.
3. Her brother rode his horse Pepper.

B. Tell which noun in each sentence below should begin with a capital letter. Then tell if the noun names a person, place, or pet.

1. Larry fished from the pond near farwell.
2. Patty kicked the ball to peter.
3. Ginny fed blaze some carrots.

> Begin the names of special people, places,
> and pets with capital letters.

Practice

A. Read these sentences. Write correctly the noun
in each sentence that should begin with a capital
letter.

1. Today gene is not here.
2. He is visiting a friend in portland.
3. He took his dog named tuffy.
4. Gene went with his brother paul.
5. He will be back in rockville tomorrow.

B. Look at the words in the box. Write correctly
each word that should begin with a capital
letter.

texas
ann
spotty
book

• **Write Sentences**   Write correctly the
sentences about Fluffy. Remember to begin the
names of special people, places, and pets with
capital letters.

fluffy is a kitten.
She lives with kathy.
They live in new york.

6 | Titles for People

Ruth was telling her friends the names of people she knows. Read what she said.

My teacher is Mrs. Hong. My principal is Miss Summers. My babysitter is Ms. Day. My uncle is Mr. Miller.

The underlined words are titles. Titles begin with capital letters. Which titles end with a period? Which title does not end with a period?

> Begin titles with capital letters. Put a period after the titles Mrs., Mr., and Ms. Miss does not have a period.

Try It Out

A. Read these sentences aloud. Tell which words in each sentence are titles for people.

1. Mrs. King gave Mr. Hunter the key.
2. Miss Kelly visited Ms. Evans.

B. Tell what is wrong with each title below.

1. miss   3. Mr   5. mrs.
2. Mrs   4. ms.   6. Miss.

7 | Days and Months

Read these signs. Look at the underlined words. The underlined words are nouns. They name a day of the week and a month of the year. The names of days and months begin with capital letters.

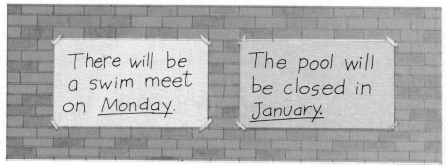

There will be a swim meet on <u>Monday</u>.

The pool will be closed in <u>January</u>.

Try It Out

A. Read these sentences aloud. Tell which words should begin with capital letters.

1. The turtle race is on saturday.
2. Will the egg race be in july?
3. The rope-jumping contest is on thursday.
4. Our art show is in april.

B. Read these signs aloud. Tell which words need capital letters.

june 12
The ball game is on tuesday.

august 5
The picnic is on saturday in Lake Park.

Begin the names of the days of the week and the months of the year with capital letters.

Practice

A. Read this sign. Write correctly the two nouns that should begin with capital letters.

Come to the apple-picking party in september. It will be on the last friday in the month. There will be games and apples for everyone.

B. Read these sentences. Write correctly the word in each sentence that should begin with a capital letter.

1. Jay's birthday is on sunday.
2. The circus is on wednesday.
3. The fair begins the first day in april.

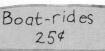

Boat-rides 25¢
Monday and Tuesday at 2:00.
Free rides on Friday at 3:00.

- **Write a Sentence**   Read this sign. Then write a sentence that tells what day you would like to go on the boat ride.

8 | Writing Months a Short Way

Sometimes we can write long words a short way. Look at the two words below. Here are two ways to write the same word.

January = Jan.

Jan. is a short way of writing January. When months are written the short way, they begin with a capital letter. They end with a period.

Most of the months of the year can be written a short way. Look at the list of the names of the months and the short way for writing most of them. Which months can be written a short way? Which months cannot be written a short way?

January = Jan.	May	September = Sept.
February = Feb.	June	October = Oct.
March = Mar.	July	November = Nov.
April = Apr.	August = Aug.	December = Dec.

Try It Out

A. Tell which month each name stands for. Use the list above to help you decide.

1. Dec.   3. Apr.   5. Sept.
2. Aug.   4. Feb.   6. Mar.

B. Tell what is wrong with the name of each month below.

1. Nov
2. jan.
3. June.
4. Mar
5. Feb,
6. aug.

> Some words can be written a short way. When you write a month the short way, begin the month with a capital letter. End the month with a period.

Practice

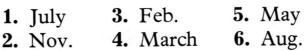

A. Write the months that have been written the short way.

1. July
2. Nov.
3. Feb.
4. March
5. May
6. Aug.

B. Write each month below the short way. Use capital letters and periods correctly.

1. October
2. December
3. April
4. September

C. Write the answers to these questions. Write the months the short way, if they can be.

1. In what month is your birthday?
2. In what month did you begin school?
3. In what month is April Fool's Day?

9 | Dates

Read the sentence below.

Men landed on the moon on <u>July 20, 1969</u>.

<u>July 20, 1969</u> is called a date. A **date** tells the month, the day of the month, and the year. The month comes first. The day of the month comes next. The year comes last.

This mark **,** is called a **comma**. A comma is used between the day of the month and the year.

Try It Out

A. Read these sentences aloud. Tell the date in each sentence.

  1. Carol was born on April 29, 1976.
  2. Dad wrote the letter on March 2, 1982.

B. Each date below is missing a comma. Read the dates aloud. Tell where the commas should go.

  1. February 22 1984 **3.** June 2 1979
  2. January 17 1987 **4.** May 30 1985

C. The dates below are mixed up. Read the dates aloud. Tell them in the correct order.

  1. May 1983 16, **3.** 10, February 1978
  2. 1980 July 22, **4.** 1977 5, October

In a date, the month comes first, the day of
    the month comes next, and the year comes
    last.
Use a comma between the day of the month
    and the year.

Practice

A. Write each date below. Put a comma where it
belongs.

1. August 4 1975 **3.** Dec. 29 1989
2. Oct. 17 1981 **4.** June 13 1986

B. These dates are mixed up. Write them correctly.

1. 4, 1976 July **3.** 1984 April 1,
2. May 1979 22, **4.** 15, 1985 March

- **Write Sentences** Write two sentences.
Sentence 1 should tell the date you were born.
Sentence 2 should tell today's date.

1. I _____
2. Today _____

10 | Holidays

You know that names of days begin with capital letters. Names of holidays are nouns. They also begin with capital letters.

Read these sentences. Look at the underlined nouns. The underlined nouns are holidays.

New Year's Day is the first day of the year.
There are many parades on Memorial Day.

Try It Out

Read the sentences aloud. Tell which nouns should begin with capital letters.

1. We saw fireworks on st. patrick's day.
2. Carl went ice skating on thanksgiving day.

> Begin the names of holidays with capital letters.

Practice

Write correctly the nouns that should begin with capital letters.

1. Please come to our labor day party.
2. Did you go to the columbus day picnic?

11 | Compound Words

Sometimes two words are put together to make one new word. A word made up of two words is called a **compound word**. Each underlined word below is a compound word.

snow + ball
dog + house

The <u>snowball</u> hit the <u>doghouse</u>.

Try It Out

Tell what two words are put together to make each compound word on the doghouse.

raincoat
tablecloth

football
watchdog
haircut

▶ A **compound word** is a word made up of two different words.

Practice

Read the story in the box. Write each compound word.

I had a great birthday! Grandfather gave me a dollhouse. I got to play basketball. I went for a ride in a sailboat, too.

• **Write a Sentence**   Write a sentence using one of the compound words from the story above.

A. Write the sentences that name another person first.

1. Alice and I went to the park.
2. I and Alice wore our yellow jackets.
3. Alice and I took our new jump ropes.
4. I and Alice played until it was time for lunch.

B. Write the noun in each sentence.

1. The wise old giant laughed.
2. One silly dragon danced.
3. All the furry monsters sang.
4. Only the spotted dinosaur whistled.
5. A muddy frog hummed.

C. Write the nouns that mean more than one in these sentences.

1. Chuck took the blocks out of the bag.
2. He made a castle with towers and windows.
3. Then he added several gates and bridges.

D. Write each sentence. Use <u>is</u> or <u>are</u> correctly.

1. The ducks (is, are) on the water.
2. A tiny bird (is, are) in the nest.
3. Two baby squirrels (is, are) by the tree.
4. The pretty butterfly (is, are) on the flower.
5. Little black ants (is, are) on the rocks.

E. Write correctly the nouns in each sentence that should begin with capital letters.

1. On monday, beth is giving a flag day party.
2. We went to maine one friday in may.
3. Did sue name the kittens blackie and lucky?
4. Is independence day always in july?
5. Mom took ted to chicago and detroit.

F. Write these titles correctly.

1. mrs   **2.** miss   **3.** ms   **4.** mr

G. Write the months that have been written the short way.

1. June   **4.** Oct.   **7.** March
2. Dec.   **5.** Nov.   **8.** Sept.
3. Aug.   **6.** May   **9.** April

H. These dates are mixed up. Write them correctly. Put commas (,) where they belong.

1. 1987 16 Feb.
2. 1982 July 24
3. Jan. 1989 28
4. 3 1978 May

I. Write the compound word in each sentence.

1. Terry helps his grandfather.
2. He plays baseball with his sister.
3. He cleans his bedroom and makes his bed.
4. He brings in the newspaper for his parents.
5. He feeds the bird and the goldfish.

1 | Getting Started

You and the children in your class tell stories about school every day. Some stories you tell together. Your class might tell the new girl about the missing turtle. You might tell the principal about the baby fish. The stories you tell together are stories you can write together.

Your class is going to write a story together. Think about the special times you have had with your class. Which ones would make good stories? Share your ideas with the other children.

The children in Mr. Ríos's class thought about their special times. They told them to Mr. Ríos. He made a list of their ideas. Here is the list.

the class puppet show

Dr. Ling's visit

our trip to the turkey farm

Write It • Make a List

A. Think about the special times you have had with your class. Decide together which ones would make good stories to write about. Tell them to your teacher.

B. Have your teacher make a list of these ideas.

2 | Choose an Idea

The children in Mr. Rios's class talked about each idea on their list. They decided together to write about Dr. Ling's visit. Each child wrote the sentence below. Then each one drew a picture showing Dr. Ling's visit.

Our class story will be about
Dr. Ling's visit.

Write It
- **Choose an Idea**
- **Draw a Picture**

A. As a class, look at each special time on the class list. Decide together which one the class will write about. Use these questions to help you.

1. Is it about our class?
2. Do we want to write about it?
3. Is it special to our class? If so, how?
4. Do we know enough about it?

Now complete this sentence and write it.

Our class story will be about _____.

B. Draw a picture showing what the class story will be about. Then take turns showing your picture to the class and telling about it.

3 | Write the Class Story

Now the class is ready to write a first draft. A **first draft** is a beginning. It is the first time a story is written. All ideas are written down.

The children in Mr. Ríos's class talked together about the things they wanted to say in their class story. They told their ideas to Mr. Ríos. He wrote their first draft for them.

Write It • Write the Class Story

A. As a class, talk together about what you want to say. Use your pictures and the questions below to help you decide.

1. Did a special person come to our class?
2. Did we go to a special place?
3. What did we see and do that was special?
4. What exciting things happened to us?

B. Help your class tell the story to your teacher. Your teacher will write the first draft for you. The class can make changes in the story later.

4 | Revise the Class Story

You and your class have written a class story together. Now help the class decide if the story is clear or if anything is missing. A good way to do this is to have someone read the story aloud. As you listen, think about these questions.

1. What parts are not clear?
2. Did we tell enough about it?
3. What parts should be left out?
4. How can we make it better?

The children in Mr. Ríos's class wrote their class story together. Then they listened as one of the children read it aloud. They talked about the questions above. They could see that some things were not clear.

The class talked about ways to make their story better. Together they decided to cross out some words and to add new ones. Mr. Ríos showed them how. He made this mark ∧ to show where to add new words. He drew a line through words that did not belong.

Look at their class story on page 47.

- Why did the class add the name Dr. Ling?
- What words were added to the story? Why?
- What sentence was crossed out? Why?

The class's revised story

> ~~She~~ ^{Dr. Ling} is a dentist. She came
> to our class with a ^giant pretend^ tooth
> and toothbrush. We laughed
> when we saw how big they
> were. Dr. Ling used them to
> show us the best way to
> brush ^our teeth^. ~~She is pretty~~.

Write It • Revise the Class Story

A. Listen as someone reads the class story aloud. Is there any part that is not clear? Did the class tell enough? Should anything be left out? The first four questions on page 46 will help you decide.

B. Talk together about ways the class can make the story better. As a class, tell your teacher what changes to make. Have your teacher cross out words that do not belong and add new ones. Decide on any other changes that will make the story better.

5 | Make a Final Copy

Mr. Ríos's class finished their story. They were proud of it, but the story looked messy. The class wanted it to look better so that people could read it easily. Mr. Ríos copied the story very neatly for the class.

Here is what the final copy looked like.

The class's final copy

> Dr. Ling is a dentist. She came to our class with a giant pretend tooth and toothbrush. We laughed when we saw how big they were. Dr. Ling used them to show us the best way to brush our teeth.

The children wanted their own copies of the class story to share. To do this, they each neatly copied the class story. Then they thought of different ways to make their copies look special.

Brett got a large piece of white paper. He cut it out in the shape of a tooth. Then he pasted his story and picture on the paper tooth. This is how it looked.

Write It • Make a Final Copy

A. Have your teacher make a final copy of the class story.

B. Make your own final copy of the class story. Use your best handwriting.

6 | Proofread the Class Story

You have made a final copy of the class story. Now you need to proofread it. **Proofreading** means you read carefully to find and correct mistakes. Ask yourself the questions below when you proofread. They will help you.

1. Are all the words spelled correctly?
2. Do all the sentences begin with capital letters?
3. Do all the sentences have the correct marks at the end?

Andrea copied the class story. Then she proofread it. This is part of what she corrected.

Andrea's story after proofreading

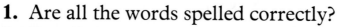

Dr. King is a dentist. She ~~come~~ came to ~~are~~ our class with a giant pretend tooth and toothbrush.

- Where did Andrea add a capital letter?
- What words did she correct for spelling?
- What end mark did Andrea correct?

Practice

Proofread these sentences. Two words need capital letters. One word is not spelled correctly. Two sentences need correct marks at the end of them. Write the sentences correctly.

1. what did Sean find.
2. Sean found hte missing wheel.
3. he found it near the slide

Write It
- **Proofread Your Copy**
- **Share Your Copy**

A. Proofread the story you copied. Use the questions at the top of page 50 to help you correct your mistakes.

B. Think of a way to make your story special.

- You can put your picture with your story.
- You can make new pictures for your story.
- You can cut a large sheet of paper into a special shape and paste your story and picture on it.

C. Share your story.

Action Words

1 | Calling for Help

The building next to you is on fire. Whom would you call for help? How would you call?

The telephone can help you in many ways. When you use the telephone for help, do these things.

1. Find the right number. Call the operator if you can't find the number.
2. Dial the number.
3. When someone answers, tell these things.

   - Tell your name.
   - Tell the address where help is needed.
   - Tell what happened.

> Use the telephone to call for help.

Try It Out

Read about the things below. They could happen to you. Tell what you should do for each one. Tell whom you should call. Tell how you would find the number. Tell what you should say.

1. Your neighbors are not home. You see someone trying to break into their house.
2. A kitten is stuck in a tree near your house.

2 | Action Words

Read these sentences. Look at the underlined words. The underlined words show action. These action words tell what Alex is doing.

Alex <u>skips</u> on the beach.
She <u>splashes</u> in the water.

Action words tell what a person, thing, or pet is doing. A word that shows action is called a **verb**.

Try It Out

A. Look at the action words on the snail's back. Choose an action word to complete each sentence. Read your sentences aloud.

1. Fish _____ in the sea.
2. Snails _____ on the rocks.
3. Birds _____ over the beach.
4. Children _____ in the waves.

swim
crawl play
climb sail
fly

B. Read each sentence aloud. Tell which word shows action in each sentence. The word that shows action is a verb.

1. Alex chases the waves.
2. The waves splash her feet.
3. She hops over shells.
4. The wind blows her hair.

> A word that shows action is a **verb**.

Practice

A. Alex wrote this story in her notebook. Read the story. Find the verbs in the story. Write them.

> I run on the beach.
> I skip over shells.
> The waves splash me.

B. Look at the picture. Then look at the words below it. Find a verb that tells what is happening in the picture. Write the verb.

flips   girl   digs   outside

• **Write a Sentence** Write a sentence about Alex. Use one of the verbs under the picture in your sentence.

Alex _____

3 | Adding -ed to Verbs

Some verbs tell about actions that are happening now. Other verbs tell about actions that have already happened.

Look at the underlined verbs in these sentences. The underlined verb in the first sentence tells about an action that is happening now. The underlined verbs in the last two sentences tell about actions that have already happened.

Ira and I walk to the beach.
We walked in the waves this morning.
We walked along the shore yesterday.

What letters were added to walk to make walked? The letters -ed are added to most verbs to show actions that have already happened.

Try It Out

Look at the sentences written in the sand. Tell which words are verbs. Then tell which verbs show actions that have already happened. Remember that verbs are action words.

I skipped on the beach.

The birds play on the sand.

A snail climbed on my toe.

56

> Add -ed to most verbs to show that actions have already happened.

Practice

A. Read each sentence. Find the verb. Change the verb to show that the action has already happened. Write the new word.

1. Grasshoppers leap into the air.
2. Worms crawl up the leaves.
3. Lions roar loudly.
4. Butterflies sail in the wind.
5. Ducks quack.

B. Write each sentence. Use the verb in the ( ) that means the action has already happened.

1. Todd and Mark (play, played) in the park.
2. They (leaped, leap) over a stream.
3. Both of them (climb, climbed) a tree.
4. They (jump, jumped) in a pile of leaves.

- **Write a Sentence** Choose one verb from the box. Change it to show that the action has already happened. Write a sentence using the new word.

bump
roll
help
spill

Adding -ed to Verbs 57

4 | Using <u>did</u>, <u>done</u>, <u>gave</u>, <u>given</u>

Some verbs are used with helping words. <u>Have</u> and <u>has</u> are **helping words**.

Read these sentences. Helping words are used correctly with <u>done</u> and <u>given</u>. Helping words are not used with <u>did</u> and <u>gave</u>.

Alex's grandma <u>has given</u> her some puzzles.
Alex and I <u>have done</u> them already.
We <u>did</u> three puzzles this morning.
My brother <u>gave</u> us lots of help.

Try It Out

Read these sentences aloud. Use <u>did</u>, <u>done</u>, <u>gave</u>, and <u>given</u> correctly.

1. A circus clown (did, done) a funny trick.
2. He has (did, done) the trick before.
3. The clown (gave, given) me two balloons.
4. I have (gave, given) one balloon away.

> ▸ Have and has are **helping words**.
> Use have and has with done and given.
> Say have done and have given.
> Do not use helping words with did and gave.

Practice

Choose the correct word from the box to complete each sentence. Write the sentence.

did	done	gave	given

1. Alex has _____ her work.
2. She _____ it to the teacher.
3. The teacher has _____ Alex another job to do.
4. Alex and I _____ the job together.

- **Write Sentences** Write two sentences about school. Use the verbs in the box. Use the helping word have in one sentence. Use the helping word has in the other sentence.

gave	given	did	done

5 | Using <u>saw</u>, <u>seen</u>, <u>went</u>, <u>gone</u>

Seen and gone are verbs that are used with helping words. Have and has are **helping words**.

Read these sentences. Helping words are used correctly with <u>seen</u> and <u>gone</u>. Helping words are not used with <u>saw</u> and <u>went</u>.

Grandpa and Alex <u>went</u> to the beach.
They <u>have gone</u> there many times.
Alex <u>saw</u> some crabs on the rocks.
She <u>has seen</u> them between rocks, too.

Try It Out

A. Use <u>went</u> or <u>gone</u> to complete each sentence. Read each sentence aloud.

1. The family ____ horseback riding.
2. We have ____ riding many times.
3. My aunt has ____ with us.

B. Use <u>saw</u> and <u>seen</u> to complete each sentence. Read each sentence aloud.

1. All of us ____ the pet show.
2. Marty has ____ the pet show twice.
3. Ty and Pat have ____ it three times.

> ► Have and has are **helping words**.
> Use have and has with seen and gone.
> Say have seen and have gone.
> Do not use helping words with saw and went.

Practice

Read Kate's story. Write all the verbs in the story. Underline the three verbs on your paper that are used with the helping words has or have. Circle the four verbs on your paper that do not use helping words.

The Zoo

Rosa and I went to the zoo. Anthony has gone to the zoo, also.

We saw lots and lots of animals. I have seen some of the animals before.

We saw a baby hippopotamus. It went into the water with its mother. Anthony has seen the baby hippopotamus in the water, too.

- **Write a Sentence**   Use the verb seen or gone and all the words on the squirrel's tail to make a sentence. Write the sentence you make.

squirrels
inside
have
the
box
the

6 | Using <u>ran</u>, <u>run</u>, <u>came</u>, <u>come</u>

Two other verbs that may be used with helping words are <u>run</u> and <u>come</u>. Have and has are **helping words**.

Read these sentences. Helping words are used correctly with <u>run</u> and <u>come</u>. Helping words are not used with <u>ran</u> and <u>came</u>.

Dad and Uncle Ted <u>came</u> to watch us race.
They <u>have come</u> to watch us often.
Uncle Ted <u>ran</u> in the track team in school.
He <u>has run</u> much faster than I can.

Try It Out

A. Use <u>ran</u> and <u>run</u> to complete each sentence. Read each sentence aloud.

1. Amy has _____ to find the goats.
2. Our dog Wolf _____ with Amy.
3. The goats have _____ into the barn.

B. Use <u>came</u> or <u>come</u> to complete each sentence. Read each sentence aloud.

1. The new student _____ from Canada.
2. She has _____ to live with her aunt.
3. They have _____ to the school fair.

> ▶ Have and has are **helping words**.
> Use <u>have</u> and <u>has</u> with <u>run</u> and <u>come</u>.
> Say <u>have run</u> and <u>have come</u>.
> Do not use helping words with <u>ran</u> and <u>came</u>.

Practice

Use the words from each box to make sentences. Write the sentences you make. Then underline the helping word and circle the verb in each sentence.

come	Julio	home	has

away	two	run	rabbits	have

- **Write Sentences** Write two sentences about animals. Use the verbs in the box. Use the helping word <u>have</u> in one sentence. Use the helping word <u>has</u> in the other sentence.

| came |
| come |
| ran |
| run |

7 | <u>don't</u>, <u>doesn't</u>, <u>isn't</u>, <u>can't</u>

do not =
<u>don't</u>

does not =
<u>doesn't</u>

is not =
<u>isn't</u>

cannot =
<u>can't</u>

Sometimes two words are put together to make a shorter word that means the same thing. The words do and not can be put together to make <u>don't</u>.

Look at the underlined words in these sentences. The underlined words mean the same thing. What two words make up the word <u>isn't</u>?

Brian <u>is not</u> here.
Brian <u>isn't</u> here.

When two words are put together to make one word, one or more letters are sometimes left out. Use this mark ' to show where a letter or letters have been left out.

Look at the words on the left. See which two words make up each underlined word. What letter or letters are missing in each underlined word?

Try It Out

Read aloud the story on the door. Tell what two words make up each underlined word. Then tell what letter or letters have been left out.

I <u>can't</u> open the door. I <u>don't</u> know where the key is. Dad <u>doesn't</u> have the key. The key <u>isn't</u> on the hook.

Sometimes two words are put together to
make a shorter word that means the same
thing.
Use this mark ' to show where one or more
letters have been left out.

Boats to
Coral Bay leave
from here.

Practice

A. Write each sentence. Use the word in the ( )
that makes sense.

1. The boat (can't, isn't) here.
2. We (can't, doesn't) go for a boat ride.
3. I (isn't, don't) know when it will return.
4. The sign (isn't, doesn't) tell us.

B. Read each sentence. Write the two words that
make up each underlined word.

1. Rachel <u>can't</u> find her ball.
2. She <u>doesn't</u> know where it is.
3. It <u>isn't</u> in her room.
4. Her friends <u>don't</u> have it.

- **Write a Sentence**   Use the words on the rock
to make one shorter word. Write a sentence
using the new word.

can
not

8 | Words That Name Noises

Some words name noises. When you say these words, they sound like the noises they name.

Read aloud the noise each animal below is making. Listen to the sound the word makes. The word sounds like the noise the animal makes.

Try It Out

Read aloud the words on the barn. Find the things in the picture that make noises that sound like those words.

Some words sound like the noises they name.

Practice

- **Write a Sentence**   The words in the picture name noises. Pick one word. Write a sentence about the picture using the word you picked.

A. Write the verb in each sentence.

1. Romeo throws the ball.
2. His puppy chases it.
3. The ball bounces over the fence.
4. It lands in the bushes.

B. Write each sentence. Use the verb in the ( ) that means that the action has already happened.

1. Randi and Tanya (plant, planted) some seeds.
2. Their mother and father (helped, help) them.
3. They (water, watered) the seeds every day.
4. They (pull, pulled) all the weeds.

C. Write each sentence. Use the correct verb in the ( ).

1. The birds have (came, come) to the birdhouse.
2. Victor has (gave, given) them some food.
3. He has (did, done) this many times.
4. Kirk (ran, run) to see the birds.
5. Kirk has (saw, seen) the birds before.
6. Soon the birds (went, gone) away.

D. Write the word from the box that means the same thing as each pair of words below.

doesn't
can't
isn't
don't

1. cannot
2. do not
3. is not
4. does not

Writing About Yourself

LAKEVILL
HOSE CO.

1 | Getting Started

Have you ever been really excited or so scared that you cried? Have you been so silly that you could not stop giggling? The special things that you have done can make good stories about yourself.

Think about some special things that you have done. Which ones have you liked telling about? You may also like writing these stories.

Sandy thought about some special things that she had done. They made good stories to tell her friends. She also thought they would make good stories to write. She made a list of these special times. Here is her list.

the contest I won

the time I was a clown

the snowman I made

Write It • Make a List

Think about the special things you have done. Which ones would make good stories to write about? Make a list of them.

2 | Choose a Story

Each idea on Sandy's list would make a good story. Sandy needed to choose the idea that would make the best story to write about. She finally decided to write about the contest she won.

Sandy wrote this sentence and drew a picture of herself showing what happened in her story.

In my story, I will write about the contest I won.

Write It
- **Choose a Story**
- **Draw a Picture**

A. Look at each special time on your list. Which idea would make the best story to write about? Use these questions to help you decide.

1. Is this special time about me?
2. What do I remember about it? Do I remember enough to write a story?
3. Why would I like to write about it?

B. Finish this sentence and write it.

In my story, I will write about _____.

C. Draw yourself in your story. Then share your picture and story with the class.

3 | Write Your Story

You have decided which story you will write. Now you are ready to write the **first draft** of your story. A first draft is just a beginning. It does not need to be perfect. Do not worry about mistakes. Just write down your ideas.

Before you write, think about what you will say. You will need to tell enough so that your readers will know exactly what happened. The questions below will help you decide what to say.

1. Why is this time special to me?
2. What did I see and do?
3. How did I feel?
4. Where did this story take place?
5. When did this story happen?

Sandy thought about what she wanted to say. She used her picture and the questions on page 71 to help her. Then she wrote her first draft. She did not worry about the mistakes she made. She just got her ideas down on paper.

Write It   • Write Your Story

A. Think about what you want to say. Look at your picture. Ask yourself the questions on page 71.

B. Write your first draft. Remember that it is just a start. You will have time later to make changes.

4 | Revise Your Story

You have put down the things you wanted to say in your story. Now read it over. How can you make your story better? Ask yourself the questions below. Think about your story. Then make any changes that will make your story better.

1. Did I tell exactly what happened?
2. What parts are not clear?
3. Does every sentence belong in the story?

Next, read your story to a classmate or to your teacher. Talk about ways to make it better. If your listener has some good ideas or if you have some new ones, make these changes in your story, too.

Sandy read her story over. She thought about ways to make it better. She decided to add a word to make it clearer. Then she read her story to Rosa. Sandy thought Rosa could help her make her story even better. Sandy and Rosa talked about the story. Sandy liked Rosa's ideas. Sandy made more changes in her story using Rosa's ideas.

Look at Sandy's story on page 74.

- What word did she add about the piece of watermelon? Why do you think she added it?
- What sentence did she cross out? Why?
- What sentence did she add? Why do you think she added it?

Sandy's revised story

I was in a watrmellun eating contest. everybody got a ~~huge~~ piece of watrmellun? Then the judge said, "Get ready. Go!" ~~I had 29 seeds in my piece.~~ i gobbled up my piece the fastest I won the blew ribbon.

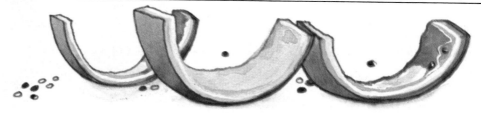

Write It
- Revise Your Story
- Discuss Your Story

A. Read your story again. Is it clear? How can you make it better? Ask yourself the questions at the top of page 73. They will help you decide.

B. Revise your story to make it better. Cross out words that do not belong. Add new ones.

C. Read your revised story to a classmate or to your teacher. With your listener, talk about ways to make your story even better. Your listener may have some good ideas. If you like the new ideas, make these changes in your story.

5 | Proofread Your Story

After you finish your story, you need to proofread it. When you **proofread**, you carefully check your writing for mistakes and correct them. Use these questions to help you proofread.

1. Are all the words spelled correctly?
2. Do all the sentences begin with capital letters?
3. Do all the sentences have correct marks at the end?
4. Have I used a capital letter for the word I?

Sandy's story was messy. She decided to copy it over. Then she proofread it.

Look at Sandy's story on page 76.

- What words did Sandy correct for capital letters?
- What words did she correct for spelling?
- What end marks did Sandy correct?

Sandy's story after proofreading

> watermelon
> I was in a watrmellun eating
> contest. ~~e~~verybody got a huge
> (E)
> watermelon
> piece of watrmellun~~?~~ Then the
> (.)
> judge said, "Get ready. Go!" ~~x~~
> (I)
> gobbled up my piece the fastest
> blue
> I won the ~~blew~~ ribbon.

Practice

Proofread these sentences. Use the questions at the top of page 75 to find the two mistakes in each sentence. Write the sentences correctly.

1. can you make a sand castle.
2. Adam and i have a new boook.
3. it tells how to make them

Write It • Proofread Your Story

Proofread your story. Ask yourself the questions at the top of page 75. The questions will help you proofread your story.

6 | Make a Final Copy

Sandy carefully copied her story in her best handwriting. Then she read it one more time. She checked it to be sure she had copied it correctly.

Sandy thought of a way to make her story look special. First she got a large piece of heavy paper. She made little stars near the edges. Then she pasted her blue ribbon and her story at the top. At the bottom, she pasted some pictures her dad took of her during the contest.

Now Sandy was ready to share her story. Here is how it looked.

Write It
- **Make a Final Copy**
- **Share Your Story**

A. Carefully copy your story. Use your best handwriting.

B. Check your story carefully. Be sure you did not make any mistakes when you copied it.

C. Think of a way to make your story look special. Share your story with your class.

Describing Things

1 | Talking About Things

When you tell about something, you can tell how it <u>looks</u> or <u>feels</u>. You can also tell how it <u>sounds</u>, <u>smells</u>, or <u>tastes</u>.

Close your eyes. Imagine you are eating your favorite food. What color is it? What does it smell like? How does it taste? What sounds do you make when you eat it? What does it feel like?

Which sentence tells more about the water?

The water feels cold.
The clear, blue water feels icy cold.

When you tell about something, tell as much about it as you can.

Try It Out

A. Look at the picture on page 78. Tell about the goat. What does it look and feel like? What sounds is it making? What is it eating? What does the apple smell and taste like?

B. Read the sentences. Which words tell how the strawberries look, smell, and taste?

Eric picked the red, juicy strawberries. They smelled sweet and tasted yummy.

2 | Words That Describe

A word that tells about something is a **describing word**. A describing word tells what something <u>looks</u>, <u>sounds</u>, <u>feels</u>, <u>smells</u>, or <u>tastes</u> like.

Read these sentences. The underlined words are describing words.

> The fire smells <u>smoky</u>.
> The <u>yellow</u> lemon tastes <u>sour</u>.
> The <u>furry</u> raccoon feels <u>soft</u>.
> The <u>big</u> lion has a <u>loud</u> roar.

Try It Out

Read this story aloud. The underlined words describe a fish.

> Danny caught a <u>thin</u>, <u>silver</u> fish.
> It felt <u>cold</u> and <u>wet</u>. Danny cleaned
> and cooked it. The fish smelled
> <u>fishy</u> but it tasted <u>good</u>.

1. Which words tell how the fish looked?
2. Which words tell how the fish felt?
3. Which word tells how the fish smelled?
4. Which word tells how the fish tasted?

> ▶ **Describing words** tell what something looks, sounds, feels, smells, or tastes like.

Practice

A. Read this story.

Joey picked up a shiny, red apple. It felt smooth and hard. Joey took a bite. It made a loud, snapping sound. The apple smelled sweet and tasted good.

1. Write the two words that tell how the apple looks.
2. Write the two words that tell how the apple sounds.
3. Write the two words that tell how the apple feels.
4. Write the word that tells how the apple tastes.
5. Write the word that tells how the apple smells.

Words That Describe   81

B. Write each sentence below. Use one of the describing words from the berry in each blank. The sentences describe the berry.

1. The berry has a ⎯⎯ shape.
2. Its color is ⎯⎯.
3. The berry feels ⎯⎯.
4. It has a ⎯⎯ taste.

sweet   blue
long   soft
    round

C. Read the sentences below. Each sentence describes a bug. Look at the words in the box. Find a word in the box that also describes each bug. Write the word.

1. This bug is round, red, and black.

2. This bug is long, black, and orange.

blue
fuzzy
spotted
muddy

- **Write a Sentence** Choose one of the words in the box above and a describing word of your own. Write a sentence about a bug using the two words.

3 | Words That Compare

Describing words can tell how things are different. Read the story about the animals running a race. Look at the underlined words.

The snake is <u>slow</u>.
The turtle is <u>slower</u> than the snake.
The snail is the <u>slowest</u> of all.

These animals do not move at the same speed. The words <u>slow</u>, <u>slower</u>, and <u>slowest</u> tell us that the animals move differently.

What letters were added to <u>slow</u> to make <u>slower</u>? What letters were added to <u>slow</u> to make <u>slowest</u>? The letters <u>-er</u> and <u>-est</u> were added to <u>slow</u> to describe the different way each animal moves.

Try It Out

A. Look at the picture. Tell a sentence about each piece of fruit. Use the words <u>small</u>, <u>smaller</u>, and <u>smallest</u>.

B. Read aloud these questions about the picture. Tell the answers.

1. Are all three pieces of fruit green?
2. Is the grape or the apple greener?
3. Which piece of fruit is the greenest?

Add the letters -er and -est to describing
words to tell how things are different.

Practice

Look at the words in each box. The words describe
the pictures below. Write the word from the boxes
that describes each picture.

big bigger biggest	

1

2

3

fast faster fastest	

4

5

6

- **Write Sentences** Write
two sentences about the
picture of the bee, owl,
and turkey. Use the
words <u>larger</u> and <u>largest</u>.

4 | Correct Order

Lynn called her aunt. This is what she did.

> She picked up the telephone.
> She dialed her aunt's number.
> She talked with her aunt.
> Lynn put the telephone back on the hook.

Look at the above sentences. What did Lynn do first? What did she do next? Then what did Lynn do? What did she do last?

When you talk about something you did, tell things in order.

When you talk about things that happen, tell them in the correct order.

Try It Out

A. This story is not in order. Read the sentences aloud. Put them in the correct order.

> Lynn got on the airplane.
> Lynn packed her clothes in a suitcase.
> She went to the airport.

B. The pictures on the right tell a story. They are not in order. Tell the story in order.

5 | Directions

When you give directions, you have two important things to do. You need to tell every step to follow. You need to tell these steps in order.

Read the directions below. They tell you every step you need to follow to cross the street safely. The steps are in order.

1. Go to a crosswalk.
2. Look to your right and to your left.
3. If the street is clear in both directions, cross the street.

Try It Out

A. The pictures below show the steps to follow to wash dishes. Tell all the steps to follow to wash dishes. Tell the steps in order.

B. The directions below tell what to do when you brush your teeth. The steps are not in order. Read the directions aloud. Tell the steps in order.

1. Get out your toothbrush and some toothpaste.
2. Put everything away.
3. Rinse the toothpaste out of your mouth.
4. Put some toothpaste on your toothbrush.
5. Brush your teeth.

C. The directions below tell how to make a cheese sandwich. They do not tell everything you need to do. Read the directions aloud. Tell what step is missing.

1. Get two slices of bread.
2. Spread the slices with butter.
3. Put the two slices of bread together.
4. Cut the sandwich in half.

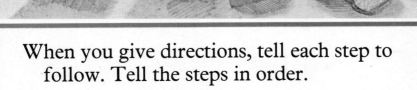

When you give directions, tell each step to follow. Tell the steps in order.

Practice

The pictures above show the steps to follow to grow carrot tops. The pictures show the steps in order. Read the steps below. They are not in order. Use the pictures to help you write them in order.

- Put the carrot tops down in a dish.

- Cut off the tops of some carrots.

- Put a little water in the dish every day for a week. See what happens.

- Put some small rocks around each top to hold it in place.

- **Write a Sentence**   These pictures show how to make celery change color. The secret is red food coloring. Look at the pictures and read the directions. Step 4 is missing. Write the missing step.

1. Fill a glass with water.
2. Put some red food coloring in the water.
3. Cut the bottoms off the celery.
4. ____

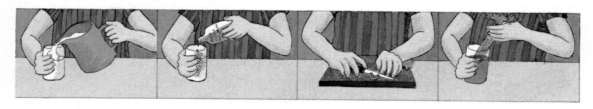

6 | Maps

Allen gave Lee a map and directions telling how to walk from Lee's house to his house. Look at the map. Find Lee's house. Then read the directions. Follow the directions on the map with your finger.

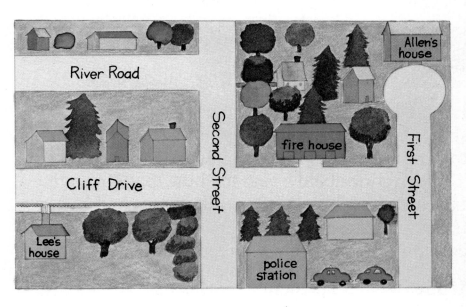

1. Turn right as you leave your house.
2. Go down Cliff Drive.
3. Go past the Fire House.
4. Turn left at First Street.
5. My house is at the end of the street.

Allen gave Lee good directions. He told her the names of the streets to follow. He told her where to turn and what she would see. He told her the directions in order.

Try It Out

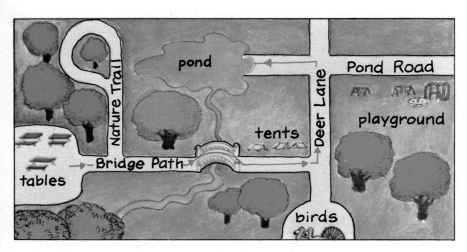

left
Pond
end
over
Street
tents
Path
Bridge

Look carefully at the map above. The blue line shows how to go from the tables to the pond. Find the tables. Then follow the blue line to the pond. The directions below also tell how to go from the tables to the pond. Read the directions and look at the map. Choose a word from the list to complete each direction. Read the directions aloud.

1. Go down _____ Path.
2. Go _____ the bridge.
3. Turn _____ at Deer Lane.
4. Go past the _____.
5. Turn left at _____ Road.
6. Go to the _____ of the road.

When you give directions, tell names and places to look for. Tell where to turn and in which direction to turn.

Practice

A. Look at the map on page 90 again. Then write the word or words in each ( ) that completes the direction.

1. To go from the playground to the birds, go down (Nature Trail, Deer Lane).
2. To go from the pond to the birds, go past the (playground, tables).
3. To go from the bridge to the playground, turn (right, left) at Deer Lane.
4. To go from the tables to the tents, walk across the (bridge, playground).

B. Look at the map on page 90 again. Then write the directions below. Use the words from the pond in the blanks. The directions tell how to go from the birds to the Nature Trail.

right
left
across
Road
Lane

1. Go down Deer _____.
2. Turn _____ at Bridge Path.
3. Go _____ the bridge.
4. Turn _____ at Nature Trail.

• **Write a Sentence** Look at the map on page 90 again. Then finish writing these directions. Tell how to get from the tents to the pond.

1. Go down Deer Lane.
2. Go past the playground.
3. _____
4. Go the end of the road.

7 | Opposites

Go <u>up</u>.

Go <u>down</u>.

The sentences on the stairs are the same except for one word. Look at the underlined words. The underlined words are opposites. **Opposites** are words whose meanings are as different as they can be. <u>Open</u> is the opposite of <u>close</u>. <u>Day</u> and <u>night</u> are opposites. What is the opposite of <u>up</u>?

Try It Out

out
sit
light
stand
dark
in

Tell which words in the box are opposites.

> ▶ **Opposites** are words whose meanings are as different as they can be.

Practice

Read the story in the rope. Write the two pairs of words that have opposite meanings.

Jeff thinks jumping rope is easy. Tony thinks it's hard. Jeff jumps quickly. Tony jumps slowly.

- **Write Sentences** Choose two words that have opposite meanings in the story above. Write a sentence for each word.

A. Read these sentences. Write the describing word in each sentence.

1. The ocean has a salty smell.
2. The dog has a loud bark.
3. The yellow bird sang a song.
4. The plum tastes sweet.
5. Our kitten has soft fur.

B. Write each sentence. Use a word from the box in each blank.

1. A swimming pool can be _____.
2. A lake is _____ than a pool.
3. The sea is the _____ of all.

deeper
deepest
deep

C. Read the directions below. They tell the steps to follow when you read a book. The steps are not in order. Write them in order.

- Close the book and put it away.
- Find a book to read.
- Sit in a nice place with lots of light.
- Open the book and read the story.

D.

Look at the map. The red line shows how to go from the lions to the monkeys. Find the lions. Follow the red line to the monkeys. The directions below also tell how to go from the lions to the monkeys. Read the directions. Choose the word in each ( ) that completes the directions. Write the directions.

1. Go down (Lion, Animal) Trail.
2. Go across the (bridge, pond).
3. Turn (right, left) at Bird Path.
4. Turn left at (Monkey, Bear) Road.
5. Go to the end of the (river, road).

E. Look at the map on page 94. Find the gate. Then follow the directions below. Answer the question.

1. Go through the gate and walk along Animal Trail.
2. Go by the bears.
3. Stay on the trail and go around the hippos.
4. Turn left at Bird Path.
5. Turn right at Monkey Road.
6. Go across the bridge.
7. Go to the end of the road.

What animals will you see? _____

F. Read the directions below. They tell what to do when you color a picture for a friend. One step is missing. Find the missing step in the box and write it.

- Get out paper and crayons.
- Think about what you want to color.
- Put your crayons away.
- Give the picture to your friend.

> Play ball with your friend.
> Color the picture.
> Write a letter.

G. Read each sentence below. Look at the underlined word. Then write the word below the sentence that has the opposite meaning from the underlined word.

1. Throw the ball over the fence.
   heavy   near   under

2. We started playing the game after lunch.
   worked   stopped   began

3. Greg speaks in a soft voice.
   sweet   hard   loud

Writing a Description

1 | Getting Started

Words can make pictures. The words <u>big</u>, <u>gray</u>, and <u>long trunk</u> help make a picture of an elephant. When you make pictures with words, you are making **descriptions**.

There are many ways to describe things. Look at these sentences.

The seeds look <u>tiny</u> and <u>brown</u>.
The mud feels <u>cool</u> and <u>wet</u>.
The air smells <u>fresh</u>.
The fish tastes <u>salty</u>.
The machine sounds <u>loud</u> and <u>noisy</u>.

Words can tell how things look or feel. They can tell how things smell or taste. They can also tell how things sound.

There are many things you could describe. You could describe something in your classroom. You could describe a special place or pet. You could even describe a best friend or the toy you like the most.

Ken thought about all the things he could describe. Then he made a list of his ideas. Here is his list.

our train set
Aunt Ruthie
my hamster Puffy
my secret hiding place

Write It • Make a List

A. Think about the things you can describe. They can be people, places, pets, or things.

B. Make a list of your ideas.

2 | Choose an Idea

Ken looked at his list. He needed to choose the idea that would make the best description. He decided to write about his hamster.

Ken wrote the sentence below. Then he drew a picture of his hamster.

The description I want to write is of my hamster.

Write It
- **Choose an Idea**
- **Draw a Picture**

A. Look at your list. Which idea would make the best description to write about? These questions will help you decide.

1. What do I remember about it?
2. Can I describe how it looks, feels, tastes, smells, or sounds?
3. Why would I like to describe it?

B. Finish this sentence and write it.

The description I want to write is of _____ .

C. Draw a picture of what you want to describe. Show and describe your picture to your class.

3 | Write Your Description

Now Ken was ready to write his description. Before Ken started, he thought about the describing words he could use. He used his picture to help him decide. Then he wrote his first draft.

Write It • Write Your First Draft

A. Before you write your first draft, think about what you are describing. What words tell how it looks, feels, sounds, tastes, or smells? Use your picture to help you decide.

B. Write your first draft. Do not worry about mistakes. Just get your ideas on paper.

4 | Revise Your Description

Your first draft is only a start. Now you need to look for ways to make your description better. Think about what you described. Look at your description and ask yourself these questions.

1. Have I told how it looks?
2. Have I told how it sounds?
3. Have I told how it feels?
4. Have I told how it tastes?
5. Have I told how it smells?

Ken looked at his paper again. He asked himself the questions above. They gave him some new ideas. He made changes on his paper.

Now Ken was ready to check with someone else. He wanted to know if he had given a clear picture of his hamster. He read his description to Doug. Doug had some questions about the hamster. Ken and Doug talked about them. When they were done, Ken had some more new ideas. He decided to make more changes on his paper.

Look at Ken's revised description on page 102.

- Ken added some words. Which word tells more about the bottle? Which word tells more about how the hamster feels?
- Ken also added a sentence. What did it tell about the hamster?

Ken's revised description

    Puffy is my hamster. She's so
soft. *and flufy* she's mostly brown except for
her white tummy, She likes to bang
her *water* bottle at nite and wake me up.
They make her cheeks puff way out.
~~I love her so much.~~

puffy stuffs seeds in her cheeks

Write It
- **Revise Your Description**
- **Discuss Your Description**

A. Read your description again. How can you make it better? Ask yourself the questions at the top of page 101 to help you decide.

B. Revise your description. Make any changes that will make it better.

C. Next, read your revised description to a classmate or to your teacher. Ask your listener for ideas for making it better. Make more changes if you like your listener's ideas.

5 | Proofread Your Description

Now you are ready to proofread your description. Read it carefully to find any mistakes. Use these questions to help you. Correct the mistakes you find.

1. Are all the words spelled correctly?
2. Do all the sentences begin with capital letters?
3. Do all the sentences end with the correct marks?

Ken looked at his paper. He thought it looked messy, so he copied it over. Then he proofread it.

Look at Ken's description on page 104.

- Where did Ken add capital letters?
- What words did Ken correct for spelling?
- What end marks did Ken correct?

Ken's description after proofreading

Puffy is my hamster. She's so
soft and <del>flufy</del> <ins>fluffy</ins>. <del>s</del><ins>S</ins>he's mostly brown
except for her white tummy<del>;</del> She
likes to bang her water bottle at
<del>nite</del> <ins>night</ins> and wake me up. <del>p</del><ins>P</ins>uffy stuffs
seeds in her cheeks. They make her
cheeks puff way out.

Practice

Proofread this story. Each sentence has two
mistakes. Use the questions on page 103 to help
you find them. Write the sentences correctly.

My coat is redd
it has five black snaps?
it keeps my warm.

Write It • Proofread Your Description

Proofread your description. Use the questions at the
top of page 103 to help you.

6 | Make a Final Copy

Ken copied his description in his best handwriting. He read it again. He wanted to be sure he had copied it correctly.

Ken thought of a way to make his description look special. He got a long piece of paper. He pasted his description on one end. Then he drew three pictures. They showed Puffy sleeping, banging her water bottle, and stuffing seeds into her mouth. This is what Ken's paper looked like.

Write It
- **Make a Final Copy**
- **Share Your Description**

A. Copy your description carefully. Use your best handwriting.

B. Read your description again. Be sure that you did not make any mistakes in copying.

C. Think of a way to make your description look special. Then share it with your class.

Working with Words

1 | ABC Order

The letters of the alphabet come in order from a to z. Words can be put in the same order as the letters of the alphabet. When you put words in ABC order, words that begin with the letter a come first. Words that begin with the letter b come next, and so on. The words in the red box are in ABC order by the first letter.

ant
bear
cat
dog

camel
chimp
cow
crow

Suppose you wanted to put the words bear and bat in ABC order. Both words begin with the same letter. When words begin with the same letter, we can put them in ABC order by using the second letter. The second letter of bear is e. The second letter of bat is a. Which comes first, a or e? Since a comes before e, the word bat comes before the word bear in ABC order. The words in the blue box are in ABC order by the second letter.

Try It Out

A. Look at each group of words below. Tell which word comes first in ABC order. Tell why. Then tell which word comes last in ABC order and tell why.

1. king   queen   princess
2. castle   tower   bridge
3. magic   secret   wish
4. mountain   forest   valley

B. The words below are not in ABC order. Tell the words in ABC order.

1. lion   duck   zebra   wolf
2. skip   hop   leap   dance
3. wink   smile   grin   laugh

C. Look at each group of words below. Tell which word comes first in ABC order. Tell why. Then tell which word comes last in ABC order and tell why. Use the second letter in each word to help you.

1. or   on   oh   of
2. fall   full   fill   fell
3. bump   bend   bang   break
4. chase   catch   crawl   climb

D. Tell these words in ABC order. Use the second letter of each word to help you.

1. fox   fish   frog   fly
2. toe   tail   trunk   teeth
3. sniff   swallow   shake   stretch

> Put words in ABC order by the first letter. When words begin with the same letter, use the second letter to put them in ABC order.

Practice

A. Write each group of words in ABC order.

1. mouse
   zebra
   toad

2. tiger
   yak
   elk

B. Write each group of words in ABC order. Use the second letter to put them in ABC order.

1. hippo
   horse
   hen

2. duck
   deer
   dog

2 | The Dictionary

Have you ever read a word, and you did not know what it meant? Did you know what to do? You could have used a dictionary.

A **dictionary** is a book about words. It tells what words mean. It shows how words are spelled. All the words are listed in ABC order. Words beginning with the letter a come first. Words beginning with the letter b come next, and so on.

If words begin with the same letter, the second letter of words is used to put them in ABC order. Words beginning with oa come before words beginning with ob. Words beginning with oc come next, and so on.

Look at this list of words. The words are in ABC order.

order
ostrich
other

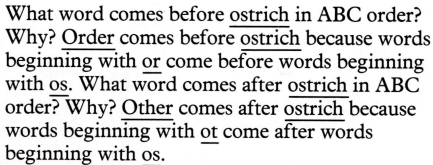

What word comes before ostrich in ABC order? Why? Order comes before ostrich because words beginning with or come before words beginning with os. What word comes after ostrich in ABC order? Why? Other comes after ostrich because words beginning with ot come after words beginning with os.

Below is a picture of a dictionary page. Look at the words in **dark letters**. What letter do all the words in dark letters begin with? Are the words in ABC order? Can you find the word **ostrich**? **Ostrich** is easy to find, because the words in dark letters are in ABC order.

order

The letters in the alphabet always follow each other in the same way. A,B,C,D,E,F,G,H,I,J, K,L,M,N,O,P,Q,R,S,T,U,V,W,X,Y, and Z is the **order** of the alphabet.

ostrich

An **ostrich** is a huge bird. It has long legs and a long neck. **Ostriches** cannot fly, but they can run very fast.

ostrich

other

1. Vicki wears two socks on her feet. One sock looks fine. The **other** sock has a hole in it.
2. Kim has no time to play today. She will have time to play some **other** day.

Try It Out

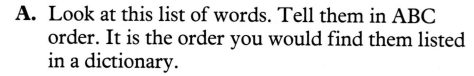

stars
sea
swim
sail
ship

A. Look at this list of words. Tell them in ABC order. It is the order you would find them listed in a dictionary.

B. Look again at the picture of the dictionary page on page 111. Tell the answers to these questions.

1. What letter do all the words in **dark letters** begin with?
2. Does the word **other** come before or after the word **order**? Tell why.
3. Does the word **ostrich** come before or after the word **other**? Tell why.

> ▶ A **dictionary** is a book about words. The words in a dictionary are listed in ABC order.

Practice

Write the words in the box in ABC order.

clown	castle	circus	chief

- **Write a Sentence** Write a sentence using one of the words in the box above.

3 | Finding Word Meanings

You know how to find words in a dictionary. Now you are ready to learn how to find the meanings of words in a dictionary.

Look again at the picture of the dictionary page on page 111. Find the word **ostrich**. There are some sentences under ostrich. These sentences tell you what the word means. Read the sentences. What does the word ostrich mean?

Now look at the picture under **ostrich**. It shows you what an ostrich looks like. A picture can help you understand a word. What do you learn about an ostrich from the picture?

Try It Out

Look at the picture of the dictionary page on page 114. Tell the answers to these questions.

1. What letter do all the words in **dark letters** begin with?
2. Does **ugly** come before or after **umbrella**? Tell why.
3. Which word means a brother of your mother or father?
4. Which word uses a picture to help you understand what it means?

ugly

Monsters are hard to look at. They are not pretty. They look mean and terrible. Monsters are **ugly.**

umbrella

An **umbrella** is made of cloth and metal. It opens into the shape of an upside-down bowl. People hold **umbrellas** to keep themselves dry when it rains.

umbrella

uncle

Any brother of your mother or your father is your **uncle.** The husband of any of your aunts is also your **uncle.** Some people have several **uncles.**

under

1. A car moves on its wheels. The wheels are **under** the rest of the car.
2. George covers his face with a mask. His face is **under** the mask.

> Use a dictionary to find the meanings of words.

Practice

Look at the words in the box. Then look at the meanings of words given below. Read each meaning. Find the word in the box that goes with each meaning. Write the word.

seat	school	shoe	salt

1. _____ This is something that people put on food. It looks like white sand.
2. _____ This is a place where teachers teach children.
3. _____ This is something to sit on.
4. _____ This is something that goes on a foot.

Look again at the words you wrote. Are the words in ABC order? If you have put the correct word with each meaning, the words you wrote will be in ABC order.

- **Write a Sentence** Write a sentence using one of the words in the box above. Use the word correctly.

4 | Getting the Meaning

trip
peanut
jeep

Read the sentence below.

> Super Berry will go on a <u>journey</u> to the moon.

The underlined word may be new to you. Do you know what it means? Sometimes the other words in the sentence will help you decide. Read the sentence above again. What word on the moon has almost the same meaning as the underlined word?

Try It Out

A. Read the sentence below. Tell which word below the sentence has almost the same meaning as the underlined word.

> The <u>module</u> landed on the moon.
>   month   spaceship   summer

flew
trip
grabbed
ran

B. Read the story below to yourself as your teacher reads it aloud. What do the underlined words mean? The other words in the sentences will help you decide.

> Super Berry <u>snatched</u> her cape off the hook. She <u>raced</u> to her rocket. She <u>soared</u> into the sky. Will this be a dangerous <u>expedition</u>?

Read the story aloud again. Use a word from the rocket in place of each underlined word.

> Use the other words in sentences to help you get the meaning of new words.

Practice

Read each sentence below. Decide which word below the sentence has almost the same meaning as the underlined word. Write it.

1. Three hawks flew high above the trees.
   hammers   dresses   birds

2. The dachshund barked and wagged its tail.
   dog   cat   drum

3. Cattails are growing near the pond.
   cups   plants   days

4. Bob will put the canoe in the river.
   boat   circus   sky

5. The new carpet in Betsy's room covers the floor.
   carrot   week   rug

- **Write a Sentence** Write a sentence of your own. Use one of the words you wrote above in your sentence.

5 | More than One Meaning

Some words have <u>more than one</u> meaning. Read the sentences below. Look at the underlined words. The underlined word is the same in each sentence, but the meaning of the word is different.

This box is so <u>light</u> that I can pick it up.
<u>Light</u> the lamp so that we can see.

In which sentence does <u>light</u> mean <u>not heavy</u>?
In which sentence does <u>light</u> mean <u>turn on</u>?

Try It Out

Read each sentence aloud. Look at the underlined word. Look at the groups of words in the box. Tell which group of words has the same meaning as the underlined word.

1. Kip has an <u>orange</u> T-shirt.
2. Caroline ate an <u>orange</u> for lunch.
3. Lisa climbed to the <u>top</u> of the hill.
4. Don made the <u>top</u> spin.

the highest place
a color
a toy that spins on a point
a kind of fruit

Some words have more than one meaning.

Practice

Read the sentences below. Look at the underlined words. Choose the group of words below each sentence that has the same meaning as the underlined word. Write it.

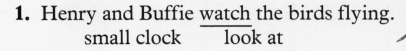

1. Henry and Buffie <u>watch</u> the birds flying.
    small clock   look at

2. Laura has a bad <u>cold</u> and has gone to bed.
    sickness   not warm

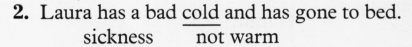

3. Painting the doghouse was <u>hard</u> work.
    not soft   not easy

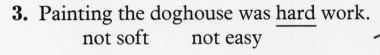

4. Dexter put the blanket in the <u>trunk</u>.
    large box   part of a tree

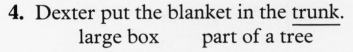

- **Write Sentences** Look at the pictures. Each shows a different meaning of <u>wave</u>. Write two sentences. Use the word <u>wave</u> in each sentence. In sentence 1, <u>wave</u> should have the same meaning as it does in picture 1. In sentence 2, <u>wave</u> should have the same meaning as it does in picture 2.

1.

WAVE

2.

WAVE

Review

A. Write each group of words in ABC order.

1. sister
   baby
   aunt
   uncle

2. ocean
   pond
   lake
   river

3. boat
   jet
   bus
   train

4. sea
   shore
   swim
   sand

B. Find the word below each sentence that has almost the same meaning as the underlined word. Write it.

1. Frank cooked the fish in a skillet.
   pan   fence   swing

2. The large, black raven flew to its nest.
   ring   hole   bird

3. Purple asters were growing in the garden.
   arrows   flowers   glasses

C. Read the words and their meanings in the box. Then read the sentences below the box. Each sentence is missing a word. Write the sentences. Use the best word from the box in each blank.

pencil	A **pencil** is something to write with.
pet	A **pet** is an animal that lives with people.
pilot	A **pilot** is a person who flies airplanes.
pocket	A **pocket** is a small bag of cloth.
puzzle	A **puzzle** is a game.

1. Manuel used a _____ to write his letter.
2. The _____ flew the airplane to Utah.
3. Nancy put the stone in her _____.

D. Read each sentence. Look at the underlined word. Write the word or group of words below each sentence that has the same meaning as the underlined word.

1. Cassie <u>beat</u> the eggs with the milk.
   hit again and again   mixed

2. Mary Beth sat down on a dry <u>spot</u>.
   place   small mark

Writing a Letter

1 | Parts of a Letter

Writing a letter is a good way to tell things to another person. A letter has several parts. Look at Sara's letter to Lori.

DATE	April 29, 1984
GREETING	Dear Lori,
	Our class did a TV show for kids. I had lots of fun! It'll be on TV in June.
CLOSING	Love,
	Sara

The **date** tells when Sara wrote the letter. Where is the comma (,)? What word begins with a capital letter?

Look at the **greeting**. It means "hello." It uses a comma, too. Where does the comma go in the greeting? All the words in the greeting begin with capital letters.

Look at the **closing**. It means "good-bye." It also uses a comma. Where does the comma go in the closing? The first word in the closing begins with a capital letter.

Sara wrote the letter. Look at where she signed her name.

Practice

Read this letter. Then answer the questions.

> June 11, 1984
>
> Dear Sara,
>
>   I saw you on TV. The whole family watched. We were so excited. Everyone liked the show. I miss you.
>
>   Love,
>
>   Lori

1. What date was the letter written?
2. What is the greeting?
3. Who got the letter?
4. What is the closing?
5. Who wrote the letter?

2 | Getting Started

Writing a letter is a good way to wish a friend a happy birthday or thank someone for a gift. You can tell about something exciting you did. You can share pictures you draw, tell jokes, or send secret messages. It is also a good way to get a letter back.

Think of someone you would like to write to. What would you like to say to that person?

Josh decided to write to Ms. Field. She was his favorite babysitter. She had moved away last summer.

Josh had a lot of things he wanted to tell Ms. Field. He also thought about the things she might like to know. He made a list of these ideas. Here is his list.

the baby giraffe at the zoo
my bird's new toy
the ice-skating rink

Write It • Make a List

A. Decide on a person to write to.

B. Think about what you want to say. What would that person want to know? Make a list of your ideas.

3 | Choose an Idea

You have made a list of things to write about. Now you need to choose one of them. Use these questions to help you.

1. Which one do I want to write about the most?
2. Which one would the person most want to know about?

Josh looked at his list. He asked himself the questions above. He finally decided to write about his bird. Josh wrote the sentence below. Then he drew a picture of his bird playing with its new toy.

In my letter, I will write about my bird's new toy.

Write It • **Choose an Idea**
• **Draw a Picture**

A. Look at your list. Decide on one idea for your letter. Use the questions above to help you. Then finish this sentence.

In my letter, I will write about _____.

B. Draw a picture of what you are going to write about. Show your picture to your class. Tell your class about it.

4 | Write Your Letter

Now you are ready to write your first draft. Just write down what you want to say. It does not have to be perfect. It is only a beginning.

Before Josh began writing, he looked at the picture of his bird. He thought about what Ms. Field would like to know about the bird. Then he started to write. He made mistakes but did not worry about them. He could change them later.

Write It • Write Your Letter

A. Look at your picture. Think about the person you are writing to. What would that person like to know? What do you want to say?

B. Write your letter. Remember that it does not have to be perfect. You can make changes later.

5 | Revise Your Letter

You have put down the things you wanted to say. Now read your letter again. How can you change it to make it better? Use these questions to help you decide.

1. What does it tell that is exciting?
2. Would I like getting a letter like this one?
3. Is there any part that is not clear?

Josh read his letter. He thought of something else to say. He made some changes in his letter.

Then Josh read his letter to Mary. He wanted to know if it was good. Mary had some new ideas. Josh and Mary talked about them. Josh looked at his letter again. He liked Mary's ideas. He used them to make more changes in his letter.

Look at Josh's letter on the next page.

- What words did Josh add? Why?
- What word did Josh change? Why?
- What word did Josh cross out and why?

Josh's revised letter

May 5 1985

dear Ms. Field,

    Do you remember _{my bird} Hooper He has a

new toy. _{It's popcorn.} I put a peace on the floor.

He hits it and makes it ~~move~~ _{jump}. Then

he chases it and hits it ~~and~~ again.

It's soooooo funny to watch.

                your friend
                Josh

Write It
- **Revise Your Letter**
- **Discuss Your Letter**

A. Read over your letter. Ask yourself the questions at the top of page 128. They will help you decide what changes to make. Then revise your letter to make it better.

B. Read your revised letter to a classmate or to your teacher. With your listener, talk about ways to make your letter even better. If your listener has good ideas or if you have any new ideas, make more changes.

6 | Proofread Your Letter

Josh's letter was messy. He copied it over. Then he proofread it. Josh used the questions on page 131 to help him.

Look at Josh's letter below.

- What spelling mistakes did he correct?
- What end mark did Josh add?
- What did Josh correct for capital letters?
- What did he correct for commas?

Josh's letter after proofreading

> May 5, 1985
>
> ^Ddear Ms. Field,
>
>   Do you remember my bird Hooper? He has a new toy. It's popcorn. I put a ^{piece}~~peace~~ on the floor. He hits it and makes it jump. Then he chases it and hits it again. It's ^{so}~~sooooooo~~ funny to watch.
>
>   ^Yyour friend,
>
>   Josh

Practice

Proofread this letter. It is missing one comma and one capital letter. It has one spelling mistake. Two sentences need correct end marks. Write this letter. Correct the mistakes.

March 16, 1987

Dear Aunt Jo

Happy birthday? I sent you a present on Monday. Did you get it yet.

love,

Ann Marie

Write It • **Proofread Your Letter**

Proofread your letter. Read it carefully for mistakes. Use these questions to help you.

1. Are all the words spelled correctly?
2. Do all the sentences begin with capital letters?
3. Do all the sentences have the correct end marks?
4. Are commas used correctly in the date, after the greeting, and after the closing?

7 | Make a Final Copy
Address an Envelope

Josh carefully copied his letter. Then he read it one more time. He wanted to be sure that he had copied it without mistakes.

Now Josh was ready to send his letter. He put his address and Ms. Field's address on an envelope. This is what Josh's envelope looked like.

Josh's envelope

JOSH'S
ADDRESS

Josh Mueller
1495 40th Steet
Westford, MA 01886

STAMP

MS. FIELD'S
ADDRESS

Ms. Jane Field
66 Main Street
Santa Fe, NM 87501

- Where did Josh place his address?
- Where did he place Ms. Field's address?
- Where are the commas in the addresses?
- What words begin with capital letters?

Next, Josh put his picture and letter in the envelope. Then he put a stamp on the envelope and sealed it. Now he was ready to mail it.

Write It

- **Make a Final Copy**
- **Address an Envelope**
- **Mail Your Letter**

A. Carefully copy your letter on a clean piece of paper. Use your best handwriting.

B. Read it over again. Check it to be sure you copied it correctly.

C. Address your envelope. Put your address in the place Josh put his address. Put the address of the person you are sending the letter to in the place Josh put Ms. Field's address. Check to see that you have used capital letters and commas correctly. Make sure the words are spelled correctly.

D. Put your picture and letter in the envelope. Put a stamp on your envelope in the place Josh put a stamp. Seal the envelope and mail your letter.

1 | Rhyme

This is a poem written just for fun. Listen as your teacher reads it aloud. Find out what the person talking in the poem will do.

Oh, Who Will Wash the Tiger's Ears?

Oh, who will wash the tiger's ears?
And who will comb his tail?
And who will brush his sharp
    white teeth?
And who will file his nails?

Oh, Bobby may wash the tiger's
    ears
and Susy may file his nails
and Lucy may brush his long
    white teeth
and I'll go down for the mail.

          – Shel Silverstein

Look again at the poem on page 135.

- A person who writes a poem is called a **poet**. The poet who wrote this poem is Shel Silverstein. Find his name. Where is it placed?
- Poems can tell us people's thoughts and feelings. In this poem, the poet tells us the things he did not want to do. What are they? Why do you think he did not want to do them? How do you think this poet feels about tigers?
- Some poems use words that rhyme. **Rhyming words** end with the same sound. Hat rhymes with cat. Sun and run rhyme. Find a word in this poem that rhymes with tail.

Activities

1. Pretend you have to tell someone how to wash a tiger's ears. What steps would you give? Make up and write directions for washing a tiger's ears. Do the same for combing a tiger's tail, for brushing a tiger's teeth, or for filing a tiger's nails.
2. Show your classmates how you would do each of the jobs above.
3. Listen as your teacher reads a poem called "My House." It has lots of words that rhyme. How many can you find? Tell them.

My House

I have in my house
A door — a floor
A rug — a mug
A stool — a tool
A book — a nook
A stair — a chair
And I'll get
I bet — a pet.

    — Jane W. Krows

2 | Rhythm

The poem below is called "Quoits." Quoits is a game. The players try to throw small hoops over a stick in the ground.

Listen as your teacher reads the poem aloud. Find out how the child talking in this poem feels about playing quoits and why. What seems strange to this child?

QUOITS

In wintertime I have such fun
When I play quoits with father,
I beat him almost every game.
He never seems to bother.

He looks at mother and just smiles.
All this seems strange to me,
For when he plays with grown-up folks,
He beats them easily.

– Mary Effie Lee Newsome

- Why do you think the child in "Quoits" has fun playing with father?
- Why do you think the father loses when he plays with his child? Do you think the child really beats father? What lines in the poem help you know this?
- When you sing songs, you often clap your hands to the beat of the music. **Rhythm** is the number of beats in the words. Listen to the rhythm of this poem as your teacher reads it again. Clap your hands in time to the rhythm.

Activities

1. Listen to the sounds around you. What rhythms do these noises have? Clap your hands or tap your feet in time with these rhythms. Compare them. How are they the same or different?
2. Sit with one or more other children. Choose an easy song to sing such as "Lou, Lou, Skip to My Lou." Sing the song together. Clap your hands while you sing. Clap in time with the rhythm. Try it once more. This time, clap out the beat without singing at all.

3 | Music

Songs are really poems, too. The poem below is a song. It is written both in Spanish and in English. Listen as your teacher read or sings the poem aloud.

Dos Y Dos Son Cuatro

(Two and Two Are Four)

Dos y dos son cuatro,
Cuatro y dos son seis,
Seis y dos son ocho,
Y ocho dieciseis.

Two and two are four,
Four and two are six,
Six and two are eight,
And eight are sixteen.

– Yucatan

Dos y dos son cua-tro, Cua-tro y dos son seis,

Seis y dos son o-cho, Yo-cho die-ci-seis.

- In Mexico, children sing this song when they are learning addition. How would this song help them?
- Children in Mexico stand in a row and clap their hands to the beat of the music as they sing the words. Clap your hands to the beat of the music as your teacher reads this poem. Listen to the rhythm. Tell how many beats you hear in each line.
- Listen to the song in Spanish. What lines end with rhyming words? Now listen to the poem in English. Do any lines end with rhyming words? Poems do not always have words that rhyme.

Activities

1. Learn the song "Dos y Dos Son Cuatro" in Spanish or English. Then find a partner. Stand and face your partner. Clap your hands together to the beat of the music as you sing the words.
2. Make up new words to an easy song. Try it with "Row, Row, Row Your Boat." Make the rhythms of both songs the same. Your new song might look something like this one.

Ride, ride, ride your bike
Slowly down the street.
Ring, ring, beep, beep,
Life is really neat.

4 | Special Poems

Sometimes poems are made in special shapes. These shapes show what the poems are about. Look at the shapes of the two poems below. What do you think they are about? Listen as your teacher reads them aloud.

- What is the shape of each poem? What is each poem about?
- Why do you think these shapes are good ones to use?
- Most poems are read from top to bottom. How do you read these poems?
- Each word in these poems is important. It helps you know what the poem is about. In the poem shaped like a flower, the word leaf tells about one of the flower's parts. The word grow tells what the flower does. What words tell how the flower looks?

Activities

1. Make a poem like the one on page 142. Think of something that you can picture that has a shape that is easy to make. It might be a tree, a bird, a fish, or a wagon. Cut or tear out words that describe the picture. Place them on a piece of paper in the shape of the thing your poem describes. Paste them on the paper.
2. Make a chain poem. Cut out 1- by 6-inch pieces of colored paper. Then think of something you can describe. Write its name on one of the pieces of paper. Now think of words to describe it. Write each describing word on a different piece of paper. Then make a chain by pasting the pieces of paper together. Hang your chain poem from the ceiling or wall.

5 | Riddles

Riddles are questions that have funny answers. Some riddles are written as poems. Their answers rhyme with a word in the poem.

Here are two riddles written as poems. Listen as your teacher reads them aloud. Can you guess their answers?

A short short tail.
A long long nose
It uses for
A water hose.

Two great big ears.
Four great big feet.
A tiny peanut
Is a treat.

Its name is El —
Oh, no! I can't!
Now you tell me:
An . . .

ELEPHANT

It has two feet,
No hands, two wings.
It can fly
In the sky.

Sometimes it chirps.
Sometimes it sings
The sweetest song
You ever heard.
Can you guess?
It is a . . .

BIRD

– Beatrice Schenk de Regniers

- In the elephant riddle, what word rhymes with elephant and helped you guess the answer?
- In the bird riddle, what word rhymes with bird and helped you guess the answer?
- Each line in the riddle also gives clues to the answers. What clues about the elephant are given in the first riddle? What clues about the bird are given in the second riddle?

Activities

1. Make up or choose your favorite riddle. Write it on a piece of paper. Draw a picture for your riddle. Share it with your class.
2. As a class, make a riddle display. Put up a large piece of paper on a wall. Write your favorite riddles on the paper. As the class finds new riddles, write them on the paper. See how many of these riddles you can answer.

Sharing Books

1 | Making a Picture Report

Sara thought the story "The Garden" from the book Frog and Toad Together by Arnold Lobel was a good one to read. She decided to share it by making a picture report. She drew pictures for the most exciting parts. She wrote something about each one at the bottom. Here are what some of her pictures looked like.

Toad shouted at his seeds. It made them afraid to grow.

Toad read a long story to his seeds so that they would not be afraid to grow.

Toad also played music to his seeds.

Then Toad fell asleep.

Look again at the four pictures on page 147.

- Tell what you found out about Toad.
- Sara was careful not to draw a picture showing the ending of the story. Why?

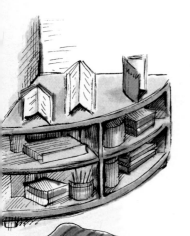

Activity

Make a picture report. Follow these steps.

1. Get some clean pieces of paper.
2. On the first piece, write the title and the author's name.
3. Think about the most interesting or exciting parts of the book. Draw a picture for each part. Do not draw a picture that gives away the ending. Only put one picture on each piece of paper.
4. At the bottom of each picture, write something that tells a little about the story.
5. Show each picture in the order it happened. Tell a little about each picture. Remember not to tell how the story ends.

More Books to Read

Night Noises: and Other Mole and Troll Stories by
Tony Johnston. This is a book of stories about
Mole and Troll. They are very good friends who do
not always get along.

Frog and Toad All Year by Arnold Lobel. This
book has five funny stories about Frog and Toad.
Frog and Toad are best friends who do many things
together.

2 | Making a Picture Postcard

Mark really liked the story The House That Nobody Wanted by Lilian Moore. He decided to share part of it by making a big picture postcard. It looked like this.

The House That Nobody Wanted by Lilian Moore

Dear Jeff,
   Here's a great book!
A man and a woman
decide to sell their old,
gray house. They want
a pretty, new one with
flowers around it. Read
the book. Find out the
ending.   Love,
          Mark

Jeff Marcum
25 Lake Road
New Castle, De 19720

- Tell what you learned about the man and the woman from the postcard.
- Tell what you learned about the house.
- Did Mark tell the ending of the story? Tell why or why not.

Activity

Make a picture postcard. Follow these steps.

1. Get a piece of heavy paper. Cut it to the size you want your postcard to be.
2. Draw a picture for the story on one side. Write the title and the author's name at the top.
3. Think of a message telling a little about the book. Do not give away the ending.
4. Write the message and an address on the other side. Put a stamp on it. Put the stamp, the message, and the address in the same places Mark put them.

More Books to Read

Bullfrog Builds a House by Rosamond Dauer. Gertrude helps Bullfrog finish building his house, but Bullfrog thinks the house needs one more thing.

Moving by Wendy Watson. Muffin wants to stay in the old house when her parents move to a new one. At the last minute, Muffin changes her mind.

3 | Making a Book Jacket

Jesse read a book called I Love Gram by Ruth A. Sonneborn. He decided to share the book by making a book jacket. He drew a picture for the book on the outside. Here is what it looked like.

I Love
Gram
by
Ruth Sonneborn

On the inside, Jesse wrote some sentences about the book. He told the most important parts without telling the ending. Here is what he said.

Ellie's grandmother was in the hospital. Ellie missed her a lot. Then, Ellie got good news. Gram was coming home. Ellie made Gram a special coming home surprise.

- Tell what you found out about Ellie.
- Tell what you learned about Gram.
- Jessie was careful not to tell the ending of the story. Why?

Activity

Make a book jacket. Follow these steps.

1. Get a large piece of paper.
2. Fold it in half.
3. Draw a picture for the story on the outside.
4. Write the title and the author's name above the picture.
5. On the inside, write some sentences about the story. Tell the most important and exciting parts. Remember not to give away the ending.

More Books to Read

Grandma Is Somebody Special by Susan Goldman. A little girl visits her grandmother. She has a good time listening to her grandmother's stories and learning about the nice things her grandmother does.

Mary Jo's Grandmother by Janice May Udry. Mary Jo goes to visit her grandmother who lives alone. When her grandmother falls, Mary Jo must go for help.

4 | Making Riddles

Carl liked reading The Secret Hiding Place by Rainey Bennett. He learned where many animals hide. He decided to share the book by writing some riddles. The riddles would give clues about the book. Here are two of the riddles.

I have black and white stripes.
I have a long tail.
My secret hiding place is in the tall grass.
What am I ?

I am big and gray. I have great big ears and a long trunk. My secret hiding place is behind leaves as big as my ears.
What am I ?

- Tell two animals Carl learned about in the book.
- Did Carl tell what animals he was talking about in each riddle? Tell why or why not.

Activity

Make a book of riddles. Follow these steps.

1. Decide what persons, animals, or things in the book you can make riddles about.
2. Think of something different or special that gives clues about each one. Also think of a question you can ask about each one.
3. Write the riddles. Write each one on a different piece of paper. Remember to ask a question at the end of each riddle. Do not tell the answer.
4. Put the pages together to make a book. Make a cover for the book. Write the title and the author's name on the cover.

More Books to Read

George and Martha by James Marshall. George and Martha are hippos who are great friends. This book has five funny stories about them.

You Look Ridiculous Said the Rhinoceros to the Hippopotamus by Bernard Waber. A hippopotamus tries to find a hiding place when she learns that other animals think she looks ridiculous. Then she has a dream.

Words for Writing

Action Words

chase
clap
climb
crawl
dance
dash
hop
jump
kick
knock
leap

march
open
play
pull
push
race
ride
roll
run
sail
scratch

shake
sing
skip
slide
splash
swim
swing
throw
trot
turn
walk

Animals

bear
cat
chicken
cow
dog
duck
elephant
fish
fox
frog
goat
hippo

horse
lion
monkey
mouse
rabbit
raccoon
sheep
squirrel
tiger
turkey
turtle
wolf

Days

Sunday
Monday
Tuesday
Wednesday
Thursday
Friday
Saturday

Describing Words

Colors	Feel	Numbers		Shape
black	cold	one	1	circle
blue	cool	two	2	flat
brown	dry	three	3	line
gray	hard	four	4	point
green	hot	five	5	round
orange	rough	six	6	straight
pink	smooth	seven	7	
purple	soft	eight	8	
red	sticky	nine	9	
white	warm	ten	10	
yellow	wet	eleven	11	
		twelve	12	
		hundred	100	

Size	Smell	Sound	Taste
big	clean	loud	juicy
fat	fishy	noisy	salty
large	fresh	quiet	sour
little	salty	ring	sweet
long	smoky	roar	spicy
short	sweet	scream	yummy
small		soft	
tall		yell	
thick			
thin			
tiny			

Directions

above
across
around
back
below
front
left
north
over
right
straight
turn

Holidays

Chanukah
Christmas
Columbus Day
Fourth of July
Independence Day
Labor Day
Memorial Day
New Year's Day
St. Valentine's Day
Thanksgiving Day
Veterans Day

Months

January = Jan.
February = Feb.
March = Mar.
April = Apr.
May
June
July
August = Aug.
September = Sept.
October = Oct.
November = Nov.
December = Dec.

People

aunt
baby
boy
brother
children
family
father
friend
girl
mother
sister
teacher
uncle

Places

city
country
farm
forest
house
mountain
ocean
pond
school
store
street
town
zoo

Titles

Miss
Mr.
Mrs.
Ms.

INDEX

Numbers in **bold type** indicate pages where item is introduced.
Numbers in *italic* indicate further practice.

Abbreviations, in months, **33–34,** *41*
Addresses, **132–133,** 150–151
Alphabetical order, **107–109,** 110–112, 115, *120*
Apostrophe, in contractions, **64–65,** *67*

Books, reporting on
    making a book jacket, 152–153
    making a picture postcard, 150–151
    making a picture report, 147–149
    making riddles, 154–155

Capital letters, used in
    addresses, **132–133,** 150–151
    closing, of letter, **123–124,** 130–131
    days, **31–32,** *40*
    first word of sentences, **10–11,** 13, 15, 17, *19,* 50–51, 75–76, 103–104, 130–131
    greeting, of letter, **123–124,** 130–131
    holidays, **37,** *40*
    months, **31–32,** *41,* 123–124, 130–131
    names, special (proper), **28–29,** *40,* 123–124, 132–133
    pronoun *I,* 75–76
    titles, for people, **30,** *40*
Class story. *See* Composition
Comma
    in addresses, 130–133, 150–151
    after closing, in letter, **123–124,** 130–131
    after greeting, in letter, **123–124,** 130–131
    in dates, **35–36,** *41,* 123–124, 130–131
Comparisons, **83–84,** *93*
Composition
    skills
        addressing an envelope, **132–133**
        parts of a letter, **123–124,** 131

steps in writing
    making a list, **43,** 69, 97–98, 125
    choosing an idea, **44,** 70, 99, 126
    writing a first draft, **45,** 71–72, 100, 127
    revising, **46–47,** 73–74, 101–102, 128–129
    proofreading, **50–51,** 75–76, 103–104, 130–131
    making a final copy, **48–49,** 77, 105, 132–133
types of
    class story, 43–51
    description, 97–105
    letter, 123–133
    writing about yourself, 69–78
See also Creative writing
Compound words, **38,** *41*
Context clues (getting meaning for words), **116–117,** *120–121*
Contractions, **64–65,** *67*
Creative writing
    book jacket, 152–153
    picture postcard, 150–151
    picture report, 147–149
    riddle, 154–155
See also Composition

Dates, **35–36,** *41,* 123–124, 130–131
Describing words, 79, **80–82,** 83–84, *93,* 97–98, 99, 100, 101–102
Description. *See* Composition
Dictionary
    finding words in, **110–112**
    finding meanings in, **113–115,** *121*
Directions, **86–88,** 89–91, *93–95*

Helping words. *See* Verbs, helping words

Letter. *See* Composition
Listening, 9, 53

Literature
  selections
    "Dos y Dos Son Cuatro" (Two and Two
      Are Four), Yucatan song, 140–141
    "Oh, Who Will Wash the Tiger's Ears?"
      Shel Silverstein, 135–137
    "Quoits," Mary Effie Lee Newsome,
      138–139
    Riddles, Beatrice Schenk de Regniers,
      144–145
  types
    music, **140–141**
    poems, **135–137**, 138–139, 142–143
    riddles, **144–145**, 154–155

Maps, **89–91**, *94–95*
Multiple-meaning words (more than one
  meaning), **118–119**, *121*

Naming words. *See* Nouns
Nouns
  defined, **22–23**, *39*
  plural, **24–25**, *39*
  proper (special names), **28–29**, 30, 31–32,
    37, *40*
  verb agreement with, **26–27**, *40*

Onomatopoeia, **66**
Opposites, **92**, *95*

Period, **14–15**, 17, *19*, 50–51, 75–76, 103–104,
  130–131

Question mark, **14–15**, *19*, 50–51, 75–76,
  103–104, 130–131

Rhyme, in poetry, **136–137**, 141, 145
Rhythm, in poetry, **139**, 141

Sentence
  capitalizing first word of, **10–11**, 13, 15, 17,
    19, 50–51, 75–76, 103–104, 130–131
  defined, **10–11**, *19*
  beginnings, **16–17**, *19*

  endings, **16–17**, *19*
  making sense, **10–11**, 13, 17, *19*
  punctuating, **14–15**, 17, *19*, 50–51, 75–76,
    103–104, 130–131
  questions, **14–15**, *19*
  telling, **14–15**, *19*
  word order in, **12–13**, 17, *19*
  writing, 11, 13, 15, 17, 18, 19, 23, 25, 27,
    29, 32, 36, 38, 44, 51, 55, 57, 59, 61, 63,
    65, 66, 70, 76, 82, 84, 88, 91, 92, 99, 104,
    112, 115, 117, 119, 126
Signs, **18**
Speaking
  about others and yourself, **21**, *39*
  giving descriptions, **79**, *93*
  giving directions, **86–88**, *93–95*
  telling events in correct order, **85**, *93*
  on the telephone, **53**
  with clarity, **9**

Telephone, using the, **53**
Titles, for people, **30**, *40*

Usage
  came, come, **62–63**, *67*
  did, done, **58–59**, *67*
  gave, given, **58–59**, *67*
  ran, run, **62–63**, *67*
  saw, seen, **60–61**, *67*
  went, gone, **60–61**, *67*

Verbs
  agreement. *See* Nouns, verb agreement with
  defined, **54–55**, *67*
  helping words, **58–59**, 60–61, 62–63, *67*
  past tense (adding *-ed*), **56–57**, *67*
  See also Usage

Words for writing, 156–158
Writing. *See* Composition; Creative writing;
  Sentence, writing
Writing about yourself. *See* Composition

160